WALKING FORWARD

Discoveries in Freedom and Forgiveness

By Arden J. Campbell

Copyright © 2010 by Arden J. Campbell

Walking Forward
Discoveries in Freedom and Forgiveness
by Arden J. Campbell

Printed in the United States of America

ISBN 9781609575953

All rights reserved solely by the author. The author guarantees all contents are original and do not infringe upon the legal rights of any other person or work. No part of this book may be reproduced in any form without the permission of the author. The views expressed in this book are not necessarily those of the publisher.

Unless otherwise indicated, Bible quotations are taken from The New King James Version of the Bible. Copyright © 1982 by Thomas Nelson, Inc. Nashville, Tennessee; and The New International Version Study Bible. Copyright © 1985 by The Zondervan Corporation, Grand Rapids, Michigan.

www.xulonpress.com

Table of Contents

Part I: Recognizing Freedom and Forgiveness

Chapter 1 – What My Cats Have Taught Me About Freedom 15
Chapter 2 – Freedom and Forgiveness – Behind the Clouds 28
Chapter 3 – Freedom Through the River of Life 34
Chapter 4 – Trapped in a Stairwell 45
Chapter 5 – Locked Doors 55
Chapter 6 – Freedom in Stillness 59
Chapter 7 – Freedom Road 63

Part II: Experiencing Freedom and Forgiveness

Chapter 8 – Collars for Healing 73
Chapter 9 – Logjams to Freedom 80
Chapter 10 – Freedom Through Surgery 85
Chapter 11 – Freedom's Sometimes Painful Limits 91
Chapter 12 – Pruning and Freedom 96

Chapter 13 – Freedom Through Experiencing Bitterness 103
Chapter 14 – Freedom Emerging Out of the Fiery Furnace 107

Part III: Life's Tests of Freedom and Forgiveness

Chapter 15 – Freedom in Brokenness 113
Chapter 16 – Freedom – Knowing the Whole Story 117
Chapter 17 – Freedom to the End 124
Chapter 18 – Freedom on the Other Side 134

This book is dedicated to:

My parents –
Who so often had to forgive me.

God the Father –
The author of freedom and forgiveness.

God the Son –
Through whom we have been given freedom and forgiveness through grace!

God the Holy Spirit –
Who breathes freedom and forgiveness in and through us!

Acknowledgements

First, thank you, Jesus Christ, for bringing me into a relationship with you at the age of 16 and continuing to pour out Your grace and mercy day by day as I walk forward in greater intimacy with You. Thank you Carol for introducing me to Joanie, who started me on this life-long journey of inner healing and deliverance from living like an orphan to thriving as a daughter of the King! Thank you to Lynn, Drew, Roger, Christie and Sue who read this manuscript and gave loving, thoughtful input. To Jill, Kathy, Marcie, Mary Jill, Eszter, Anita, Gabi, Barb, Larisa, Lea and Tom: I cannot say thanks enough for your patience, perseverance and prayers with and for me, always pointing me to my very Best Friend! To Donna, thank you for the "knock-out" word from the Lord for me. Thank you to all those mentioned in these pages who have played such powerful and significant roles in my life in the forgiveness and freedom journey.

Introduction

We all want, in the very core of our beings, to experience true freedom; freedom from shame, guilt, our own mind-games, and freedom to live in the joy and peace that only comes in an intimate relationship with the living God. I lived a good part of my life with Jesus thinking that if I simply studied the Word of God more, was discipled well, served the Lord, and poured my life into others that freedom would unfold and grow. That didn't work. I am only now learning that a major key to freedom is forgiveness, and more importantly, intimacy with Jesus, the author of forgiveness.

This is a book about journeying through life's every day situations and experiencing the touch of God in them. Embarking on any journey means taking steps forward and walking into the unknown. In that place, quite often, the Holy Spirit will encounter our hearts in new and fresh ways with His Truths.

So, if you are looking for a book that gives one person's personal, real-life experiences and how God revealed Himself and some truths about freedom and forgiveness to her through those experiences, then this is your book!

My hope is that the Spirit of the living God will somehow use what is written in these pages to encourage you and lead you to explore and be open to the ways He speaks to you through your everyday experiences in a fresh way. In addition, I pray it draws you into greater intimacy with God. You may not be able to relate to any of the specific experiences I have had, but you might connect with some of the lessons and truths which have emerged from them. Lord willing, my prayer is that you can apply the Truth of His Word to your situations, whatever they may be and know that indeed, God *is* good, and *all* He does and allows is for our good and our transformation into the image of His Son, Jesus, and ultimately, for His glory. Surely, He intends for us to walk in freedom and forgiveness all the days of our lives, embraced by Him in His great, abiding and unconditional love!

Arden Jan Campbell

Part I

Recognizing Freedom and Forgiveness

Chapter 1

What My Cats have Taught Me About Freedom

Part I: Love's Power to Break Through Stony Hearts

You have probably already noticed that this is the longest chapter, and that is largely because I've had my "boys", Toby and Simon, for over twelve years now, and they have taught me a great deal about freedom as well as about love. Thus, this is an appropriate place to start this section entitled "recognizing freedom."

Actually, I grew up a dog lover and really didn't think much about cats, except that a friend's cat had once bitten my ankle when I was about twelve years old. So, when I was in my 30s and a friend suggested I get a couple of cats, I had to spend some time thinking about it. In the end, I thought I'd get one kitten—that would be plenty. So, my friend, Heather, and I went off to the SPCA to purchase a kitten from "kitty-city". There must have been thirty kittens running around this room made just for them, and as we sat looking at, petting and holding the many kittens vying for our attention, I noticed one "larger" grey kitten with the longest legs I'd ever seen, walking slowly on the opposite side of the room. Suddenly, I saw him start to gag and wretch and then throw-up. I stated right then and there that I was definitely NOT getting that kitten. Oh, God has such a sense of humor!

About two minutes later, that same puking, grey kitten sauntered over to me, crawled up in my lap and promptly fell asleep! I looked at Heather, who said, "He's the one!" and even as I protested, my heart was drawn to this little guy who obviously had fallen in love with me already. So, reluctantly, I took this long-legged, puking kitten home, named him Toby, and tried not to let my heart get too attached.

You see, he wouldn't eat, or rather couldn't eat. After about two days, my cat-lover friend said I needed to get some kitten milk replacement and an eye-dropper and feed him by hand until he gained strength and could eat on his own. Honestly, I didn't want this kitten anymore—he was too much work, and hadn't I gotten him for pleasure, not for me to be a nurse-maid? I kept asking myself why I'd agreed to buy this ill kitty? Why didn't I get a lively one? I began to make plans to take him back to the SPCA and choose another one, but something the woman working there said to me on the day I purchased Toby made me pause and reconsider. "Oh, I'm so glad you are getting this little guy because he was scheduled to be put down tomorrow!" Something in me cried out, "I can't let him die!" Isn't this entire scenario just like our Heavenly Daddy? He sent His precious son, Jesus, to seek and save the lost, to heal the sick and broken-hearted and cries out over every person, "I don't want you to die!"

To make a long story short, these times of feeding Toby with an eye-dropper turned into precious hours of "bonding" between me and Toby as I would hold him just like a little baby. He looked up at me with his huge green eyes, and his front paws would grip my hand as I fed him. Then he would slowly grow sleepy, and I would sit down in my easy-chair and just hold him as he slept. We would sit this way for probably thirty minutes every day a few times a day, and as Toby slept, I would pray, and the Lord began opening up my heart to His love for me. I sensed deep in my spirit that the God of the universe held me like this, all the time, and just loved on me. Plus, I quickly realized in new and deeper ways that love is all about giving.

Oh, I already knew the Lord; I'd been a follower of Jesus for years, but there were numerous blockages in my heart that God was showing me that were keeping me from receiving and giving love. God was beginning to chip away at my heart of stone, pour out His love into me, and He was using a sickly kitten to do it.

Of course this was just the beginning, and it would take years for His surgical "chippings" to break through a very stony heart so I could receive

His love. Sitting there loving on this little kitten was the first step of many with Toby, and later with my second cat, Simon, of learning about love and freedom!

Part II: The Religious Spirit Rears Its Ugly Head

Toby quickly gained strength and began to play, do summer-saults, run, chase balls and truly live! He was a talker from the beginning, loudly exclaiming his presence, pleasure or desires. I realized very quickly that Toby the talker was also very social and needed a playmate. So, I was off again to kitty-city to find another kitten and buddy for Toby.

I brought Simon home and after going through the days of getting them accustomed to one another, they were fast friends and playmates, a good thing since I was gone for many hours each day at my job.

I know I am jumping way ahead, but the lessons in freedom the Lord began teaching me through my cats only truly began after I and my boys moved to Szeged, Hungary two years after I'd gotten them. Oh, the airplane ride was an adventure in itself, and after arriving, both I and my boys began getting used to living in a new home and new country.

Toby and Simon had been primarily indoor cats (still with claws) in Virginia, with short, monitored excursions outside, and when I got to Hungary, I determined that they would remain exclusively indoor cats for a number of reasons. First, I lived in an apartment building and there were two other apartments on my floor, and the people living in them would often leave their front doors open for fresh air flow. I did not want to disturb my neighbors with unwanted visits from my cats. Second, there were about seven cats who regularly wandered into our courtyard area downstairs, and I did not want to see World War III breaking out between my cats and the neighbor cats. Finally, I had learned that indoor cats are much healthier, cleaner, and live longer. These were all very good, logical reasons to keep my cats inside.

Well, my boys quickly learned how to stand close to the front door as I would prepare to leave and would do their best through voice and body pushing to break free and escape their indoor confines. I continued to "insist" that they stay inside, and the few times they did escape, they of course went dashing into one of my neighbor's apartments; so I would run in and apologize profusely for their "behavior". My neighbor, Kati, said it was perfectly ok, and she began to fall in love with both Toby and Simon, coming over to visit me and them almost daily. Finally, she said, "Why don't you let them out on the balcony? I don't mind if they come in my house, really!" This was the first step of freedom for them, and indirectly for me, as I would open the door and both of them would go streaking out of my house onto the walkway balcony, and of course, into Kati's apartment.

It was clear that they were much, much happier about having this taste of freedom. The patient chipping away at my heart continued. I still didn't want to let them down into the yard below, and they would stare with great wonder and desire at all the cats gathering below, aching to be a part of the party! Now the challenge became keeping them from getting into the stairwell, which led down into the yard below, and all the "dangers" that lay outside! I remember thinking, "I wish I could communicate to them that it is dangerous for them to go outside into the yard. Those cats could have diseases they could catch. They could get in a horrible fight, which would mean trips to the vet. They could get ticks and fleas. Being 'limited' but a little bit free is the very best thing for them! I know what is best for them, and limiting their freedom is clearly the best option."

    I honestly thought that this too was a spiritual truth. God puts limits on us and guidelines to keep us from moving into danger or getting hurt. Now of course there is some truth to this; God does indeed protect us, and has given us His Word and the Holy Spirit as a "check" for us; but how quickly I was able to get very legalistic and religious in my "interpretations". Of course when these spirits show up, control begins to creep in and dig its claws into our souls— what tremendously deceptive spirits. Oh, how little I understood about freedom, but how patiently the Lord worked with me and continued lovingly chipping away.

Part III: God's Patience in Breaking Through Religiousness

This new freedom Toby and Simon had was actually incredibly labor intensive for me. Whenever I wanted or needed to leave, I had to track them down on the balcony or at my neighbor's flat and carry them back to my flat to lock them in. I finally learned to leave my front door ajar when I was home, even in the winter months, to allow them free passage.

Finally, after six years of living in that apartment, I developed a brilliant idea. I cut a corner out of the mosquito screen in the kitchen window so that they could go in and out of the house and onto the balcony when I wasn't home! Oh, this made Toby and Simon so happy, granting them just a little more freedom. The question that plagued me was, "Why didn't I think of this idea years ago?" I believe the Lord spoke the following very clearly to me:

"You have your way of looking at things, your way of managing life, of controlling your life and even those around you, not just Toby and Simon. You are stubborn and prideful. You believe that your way is best because it is 'easiest' and most manageable for YOU. However, this isn't love, nor is it loving, nor is it true freedom. It's YOUR version of freedom… it's a freedom YOU can manage and control, but in doing so, you are robbing Toby and Simon of their inborn freedom. And don't you see that this is simply a reflection of your own life and your own theology? You are limiting the freedom you yourself could experience in Me because you have your ways of believing, which are not truly open to my Holy Spirit working in your heart, mind, soul and spirit."

This revelation was like a violent punch in the stomach. I wish I could write that everything radically changed immediately. It didn't. I began letting Toby and Simon into the stairwell, affording them the next step of freedom, and hoping that this would satisfy their longings to be free. However, what happened was that they started to urinate and defecate in the stairwell, marking it as "their" territory, and as a result, they also began "marking" their territory on the balcony and even in Kati's and my flats. This was not what I expected in granting them more freedom, and of course I tried to "do the right thing" and purchase spray that would calm them and keep them from marking.

How often do we think of human interventions, cloaked in "spiritual terms" rather than submit to the Holy Spirit and allow Him to show us the best way? This spray "sort of worked" but again was very labor-intensive, and expensive, not to mention the time, effort, and energy I had to put into cleaning up cat urine! Isn't that the way it is when we try to take charge over situations, even thinking that this is what the Lord wants, without truly inquiring of Him, seeking His answers, and releasing it all into His hands to do it His way? Doing it "our way" can be very expensive, both monetarily and spiritually, as well as physically, emotionally and relationally.

My boys still longed for complete freedom, which took another year and intervention from the outside to accomplish.

Part IV: Completely Out of Control and Loving It!

I left for the U.S. in the summer of 2007 for a few weeks, leaving my neighbor Kati "in charge" of taking care of my cats. When I arrived back in Hungary and opened the door to the courtyard, I was greeted by my Toby, tail sticking straight in the air and running toward me across the grass from the far end of the enclosed, courtyard. Simon was close behind him, and I couldn't believe what I was seeing! My first reaction was shock, then disbelief that Kati had clearly "disobeyed" my instructions. Then, as Toby flopped over onto his back, begging me to rub his belly, the last vestiges of hardness and coldness in my heart melted. I dropped my bags on the concrete, and in that instant, I dropped the burden of control.

I clearly saw, both physically and emotionally, how happy my boys were to be free and able to roam in the yard. I quickly looked around for the neighbor cats, none of whom were to be seen. Kati informed me that it didn't take long for Simon to chase all of them out of the yard, and they don't come into our yard when my boys are there.

I certainly could not be angry with Kati, although I felt like I wanted to be. As she explained to me how incredibly happy and content they are and how they'd stopped marking territory inside the stairwell and our flats, it dawned on me, after seven years, that complete and total freedom is exactly what my boys have needed all along. Why had it taken me so long to recognize this?

Blindness is a devastating thing, whether physical or spiritual, and when God heals it, the weight that lifts off one's heart and the subsequent freedom in the Spirit that enters in is inexplicable! It must be a bit like Lazarus felt when he emerged from the tomb after having been dead for four days and was raised to life by Jesus, who told the people standing there to "take off the grave clothes and let him go." (John 11:44 NIV)

From the beginning, God intended for us to live in utter and total freedom, in a loving, trusting relationship with Him and others; however, we gave it away, and since then, have had to relearn what it means to be free.

There was one more step to freedom that needed to happen, and that it took me seven years to figure this one out simply amazes me. I finally purchased and had installed a cat door! Now my boys could freely go in and out of my flat through the cat door, thus saving money on winter gas bills! Year seven has truly become the year of jubilee for me as my boys are finally free and God has shown me that so am I!

All the limitations I put on them I justified, thinking I was protecting them, keeping them from harm, and doing what was best for them, when in reality, I was robbing both them AND me of true freedom! I used to worry about my cats a lot...would they get ill? Would they get into a fight and get injured? Would they leave the yard and wander away and get lost or stolen? The answer to all of these questions is a resounding: Yes, quite possibly all these things could happen, but SO WHAT? Simon refused, about four times, to come in when called in the evening, and spent those nights outside, once in pouring rain. Kati was much more concerned than I was, taking her flashlight outside to look for him, even though I told her, "forget it...he'll be fine, and even if he isn't, oh well. It's his choice."

Friends have asked me if I really mean that, and amazingly, I do. I don't fully understand what has happened in my heart; the only thing I can understand is that grace, peace and joy has settled into the depths of my heart and continues to grow as I surrender to the Lover of my soul and the true giver of freedom, Jesus Christ. This is freedom. This is love. Giving freedom to my cats has shown me in a tangible way the freedom that God has given each one of us, if we want to embrace it fully.

The one thing, I believe, that keeps us from living and walking in His freedom is fear. Fear is the opposite of freedom. Fear binds up everything: mind, body, heart, spirit and soul. God's perfect love drives out all fear! (1 John 4:18 NIV) Because of who He is, we are free. He purchased our freedom on the cross that we would live in His love, freely receiving from Him, freely giving that love to others so that they can be all that God created them to be!

Part V: Stony Hearts Broken Wide Open

Will I make mistakes in my new-found freedom in the Holy Spirit? Probably. But so what? God is the one in control! However, as I walk in closer intimacy with Jesus, which is what I was created to do, and listen intently to the Spirit through His Word, in prayer and in my spirit, I grow in increasing freedom to see and hear from Him more than ever, solely because of His loving grace. The spiritual boundaries I set for myself, just like those I set for my cats, appeared to be good limits, safe limits, boundaries that would keep me and others "functioning" well and within the confines of my "understanding" of who God is through His Word. Yet God says, "Trust in the Lord with all your heart and lean not on your own understanding." (Proverbs 3:5 NIV)

The step-by-step freedom that I afforded my cats is similar to the step-by-step process God, in His grace and mercy, has led me through in experiencing freedom in His Spirit. And just as radically shocking as it was for me to see my boys running freely to me across the yard, it was shocking for me that God came racing to me, His prodigal daughter, completely broken through a variety of situations, losses and events.

He ran to me, His daughter, formerly trapped by religiousness and pharisaical beliefs and actions. He wrapped His arms around me, spoke words of love and forgiveness, gave me the robe of His Holy Spirit, and danced with me all the way back to His house as I wept. I still weep, and rest in His grace, peace and unfathomable love for me and in the freedom to be His precious daughter!

Questions to consider:

1. What are some life-markers you can point to in your journey toward freedom in the Lord? *Getting baptized 2.*

2. Ask the Holy Spirit to show you what "religious" beliefs you have held fast to your whole life which may actually be keeping you from walking in freedom. *Eating alot and that's not good, but I'm doing good now.*

Chapter 2

Freedom and Forgiveness... Behind the Clouds

The day started out brilliantly, with just a few puffy clouds gently resting on the peaks of the mountains in the distance. Shorts, boots, t-shirts, sunglasses and walking sticks ready with backpacks stuffed with rain gear—we were set for our long day of hiking to the remote hut that has no electricity, but would be our home for the night.

In Switzerland, the weather is changeable by the quarter-hour and sure enough, just fifteen minutes into our walk, heavier clouds and fog began to descend, obscuring the magnificent view of the still snow-capped peaks in the distance. A short time later, the rain began to fall as the valley floor we were traversing became a thick wall of fog and rain. Emptying our packs and donning all the rain-gear available, we braced ourselves for the long journey upward and ahead, which would prove to be exhausting and one which would leave us soaked to the bone.

At various points along the rather slippery, steep and at times, treacherous path, the clouds would break and the sun would skirt through, lending a warmth and brilliance to the rain soaked leaves and flower petals lining the trail. Almost as quickly as the sun would come screaming through, the clouds, fog and mist would again come rolling in, plunging us into the coolness of yet more rain and obstructed views.

We could hear the roar of, what we were told, were majestic waterfalls all around us, but we could not see them because of the fog. Somewhere out there was something beautiful, something freeing, something that EVERYONE would want to see and experience first-hand.

Five hours later, as we struggled to the top, shoes soaked with water and squishing with every step, legs screaming from the strain of the uphill climb, breaths more labored because of the higher altitude, we wondered if it would all be worth it. At every turn, I found myself growing increasingly weary, until I finally found myself saying at every switch-back on the trail, "Jesus, give me your strength, Jesus I can't make it without You!"

The Swiss flag atop the flagpole, after six hours of hiking and then turning the final switch-back, was the most welcome site of the day as it emerged through the rain and fog and clouds! As we arrived in our room and unloaded our backpacks, truly looking forward to putting on warm, dry, clean clothes, we discovered that nearly everything in our packs that was not wrapped in plastic was soaking wet; no dry clothes for me that night. At the same time, as we hung out things to dry, the clouds began to break. This time, however, it was a full break-through—not only was the fog lifting, but also the sun was shining brightly and the clouds were dissipating. Jagged, snow-covered peaks and roaring waterfalls stretched before us as far as the eye could see, reaching down into lush, green valleys and stretching upward to the afternoon blue skies above!

The clarity of this object-lesson was almost overwhelming—we must be willing to unpack the ruined, soiled, soaking "stuff" we so vainly cling to and put our hope in and bring them out into the presence of God's healing light and love so that His freedom and forgiveness can bring forth all he intends, and He can reveal His glory in our lives and all around us!

Nearly awestruck by the beauty which lay before us, my friend and I simply sat down on a bench outside and drank it all in, allowing it to penetrate the very depths of our weary bodies and even our weary souls. The sun began to warm our damp, chilled bodies and dry our wet clothes.

"Isn't it interesting," my friend broke the silence, "how all of this beauty has been there all along, but because of the rain, fog and clouds, we couldn't see it?" And there was nothing we could do to change the situation.

How true this is in our lives as we journey with God. Things can change quickly, sometimes without warning, clouds come rolling in and bring not only rain but also fog, and our vision of true freedom and forgiveness — — which is REALLY there and truly real, is obscured. Often, there is nothing we can do to change our circumstances. This can lead to frustration and discontent. We may hear beautiful words about the living water, about living in freedom, and we may even catch glimpses of it along the way. We can hear that forgiveness is the key to freedom, but somehow the pain and cloudiness of the here and now drowns it all out.

Sometimes, however, when the path becomes steep, rocky, slippery, even dangerous, and maybe the joy in the journey begins to fade, we find ourselves crying out like I did, "Jesus, I have no more strength! I cannot go on!" If we look to ourselves and our own strength to live out this life with God, we are destined for exhaustion and burn-out. Only God, through the Holy Spirit—as we finally surrender, finally come to the end of ourselves and our own strength and cry out for His strength—only He can live this life in and through us and bring us to that welcoming flagpole!

"For by grace you have been saved through faith, and that not of yourselves, it is the gift of God, not of works lest anyone should boast." (Ephesians 2:8-9 NKJV)

We sat on the bench and literally watched the rain, fog and clouds blow away and the sunshine and landscape burst forth declaring the reality that not only is God the creator of it all, all freedom and all forgiveness, but He is the only One who can bring forth His freedom and forgiveness in our lives. Like my friend and I sitting on that bench at the top of a mountain trail just being, each of us is called just to *be* in relationship with our heavenly Daddy through Jesus Christ.

"Father, I desire that they also whom You gave Me may be with Me where I am..." (John 17:24 NKJV)

When we rest in Him and live in a love relationship with Him, He will bring forth the freedom and forgiveness that flow straight from His grace and love. We are free to cast off everything onto Him, and when we do, the beauty of all He is and does shines forth more brilliantly than we could ever imagine!

"Come to me, all you who are weary and burdened, and I will give you rest. Take my yoke upon you and learn from me, for I am gentle and humble in heart, and you will find rest for your souls. For my yoke is easy and my burden is light." (Matthew 11:28-30 NIV)

The clouds, fog and rain last only for a season—and these may seem to hide the beauty of living in freedom and forgiveness, but it's all still there, unmoving and unchanging. They will burst forth into our spirits and souls as we walk in intimate relationship with the One who knows us best, and as we allow Him to unpack and heal the seemingly ruined things in our lives.

Questions to consider:

1. What are the things that are obscuring your view of God, of life, of others?

Walking Forward

2. What do you think it means to live by faith and not by sight?

3. Are you willing to ask the Holy Spirit to show you the "ruined" parts of your life and come in and heal them? Ask Him now.

Chapter 3

Freedom Through the River of Life

Brilliant sunshine and summer warm temperatures greeted us the morning after the hurricane had hit Virginia, and by 9 a.m., I was on the phone with my friends, planning our tubing trip for later that day. Now, you would think that three university educated women, all with Masters Degrees, would know that going tubing down the flood swollen waters of a river after a hurricane is not a good idea. However, the adventure and challenge awaited us, and so we donned our swimsuits, brought our water bottles and sandals, picked up our inner tubes at the local gas station and set out to go tubing.

We parked one car at the end of our planned river float, and drove my car up to our put-in point, noticing all along that the river was running pretty swiftly, and was unusually "full" of dirt, silt and yes, tree branches. Funny what a hurricane will dredge

Walking Forward

up. We reached our launching point, a narrow but fairly fast moving section and discussed whether this was a good idea or not. "Let's give it a try and we can always pull out later on downstream," we all agreed. My friend had brought a small rope which we sort of strung between us to keep us together as we floated, but it soon proved to be rather useless as the currents tossed us to and fro, first together, then apart.

We reached the end of the relatively calm section of this particular tributary, where it flowed into the larger river and we had to climb out of the river and ford our way to the edge of the main river where we would put in for the ***real*** tubing. Now that we were warmed up and felt pretty confident, we decided to go for it. The normal width of the river was probably about fifteen yards across, but today, it was rushing at about thirty to fifty yards at various points. Right then it should have clicked in that we were very ill-prepared and even stupid to attempt going down this river in our swimsuits and flip-flops on inner tubes! Whether it was stubbornness, stupidity or pride, or a combination of all three, I will never know, but instead of making the wise decision and climbing the bank up to the road and calling it a day, we put our tubes in and started down the flood waters.

It didn't take long before we were being swiftly swept downstream by the currents, unable to control what direction we were heading in. The current was taking me straight toward a downed tree, whose branches were pointing directly upstream. I tried, fruitlessly, to put my sandaled feet out and push away from the branches when my inner tube exploded beneath me, sending me straight down into the water. When I surfaced, my two friends were floating ahead of me, asking if I was ok. I said, with only a little panic in my voice, "Yea, I'm fine...let me catch up with one of you!" as I spied the boulders and rapids just ahead in the river. Neither of them was able to slow down, and I realized that I would be going through the rapids, on my own, no life-preserver, no tube, and trying, quite fruitlessly, to employ the tactics I'd learned in years past about keeping my feet facing downstream.

Thankfully, I knew how to swim, and I also knew how to pray and I was doing both frantically at this point, repenting for my stupidity and hoping against hope that I would come out of this ok.

Ahead I could see and hear the roar of rapids. I was completely unaware of where my friends were at this point, trying desperately to keep my head above water and not slam my head against branches and rocks. I spied a huge boulder right at the start of the rapids which I could see had a large crack in it. So, I made my plan. I would jam my hands into that crack and let the flow of the river catapult me up onto the side of that boulder. Then I would pull myself out of the river before tumbling down the rocky rapids. I began to swim hard toward the boulder, but the flooding currents were starting to take me away from it. I managed to grab hold of the crack and hang on as the river slammed my torso and legs into the boulder; my head was half-way under water and there was no way I would be able to pull myself out. I heard one of my friends scream at the top of her voice, "Arden, let go of the rock!" This was the LAST thing I wanted to do; I felt like that rock was my savior, my life-line, my only hope. But she saw things differently, and as my strength began to ebb, I did what she said, and the currents dragged me down into the rapids and under the water where I was tossed like a rag-doll.

I couldn't touch the bottom, and I simply flailed about trying to reach the surface, which I finally did after I don't know how long. I breathed in life-giving air, only to end up with a nose and mouthful of water, and then was dragged down again by the current. Again I flailed, arms and legs desperately searching for something stable to stop this out-of-control ride. I surfaced again, coughing out water and trying to breathe in air, only to suck in more water and be sucked under the surface again. It was at this point that I consciously realized I was drowning.

I'd often heard it said by near-death experienced people that your life flashes before your eyes before you are going to die. Well, that happened to me! I began to see important events, in colorful pictures, times in my life right there before my eyes! "I'm dying!" I thought to myself and struggled one last time to the surface, coughing and again, taking in more water than air and was dragged down again.

It was at that moment, when I felt I was a complete goner, that in my spirit I cried out, "Jesus, save me!" and immediately, my right foot hit the bottom of the river! I grasped desperately with my foot at the rocky bottom, trying to get my left foot over to where my right foot dragged along the bottom, when suddenly I stood up in the middle of this raging river, in water waist-deep, and coughed and gasped for air.

"I waited patiently for the Lord; he turned to me and heard my cry. He lifted me out of the slimy pit, out of the mud and mire; he set my feet on a rock and gave me a firm place to stand." (Psalm 40:1-2 NIV)

In utter shock and definite delirium, I realized that one slip and I'd be tumbling down the river again, so I stood there and prayed, "Jesus, help me!" I looked to my right and about ten feet away was a large boulder near the river bank. I fixed my eyes on that boulder and slowly started moving toward it, crying out to the Lord to keep my feet firm and not let me slip.

When I reached the boulder, I plopped face down in utter exhaustion, on this boulder and started laughing hysterically with tears rolling down my cheeks simultaneously. One of my friends came running down the bank screaming, "Are you ok? Omigosh, when you let go of the rock, you disappeared and I never saw you come up again! I thought you were gone!" I couldn't even answer her; I was in such a state of shock.

Miraculously, I had just two minor cuts on my legs and a bad strawberry burn across my thigh, but no other injuries after having been pummeled by branches, rocks and other debris. Our other friend had lodged herself in a tree in the middle of the river. There she half-sat, half-stood, clinging to the tree with one hand and to her tube with the other. She was terrified.

After I'd recovered a bit, we instructed her as to exactly what she needed to do...she wouldn't be able to get to our side of the river, but could get to an alcove on the other side. This was the last thing she wanted to do. We spent about fifteen minutes calming her and convincing her that she could do it. I prayed as she leapt off the tree and into her tube and swam desperately for the shore, grabbing hold of a downed tree trunk at the mouth of the alcove. The current was pulling at her tube where her legs were clinging, and we screamed at her to let go of the tube; when she did, she was able to pull herself to shore on the opposite bank.

"Let go of the rock!"

"Let go of the tube!"

Are we willing to ask God to show us any worthless idols we may be clinging to so that He can expose them, we can repent, and finally be set free?

About one minute later, three kayakers came gliding down the river and saw our dilemma. Helmets on, life-preservers, properly equipped boats with water skirts, and strong oars were worn by each one. We ill-equipped three looked pretty bedraggled and pitiful, but these kayakers took pity on us and were able to bring our friend from the other side of the raging river to where we were. They asked us what we were doing, and when we said, "Tubing down the river," they looked at us incredulously, and said, "Well, be careful!"

After the three of us reunited, having lost two inner tubes now, the one friend who had not yet personally endured any sensational experiences on the river suggested that we all cling to the one remaining inner tube and continue on down the river! I could not believe she would even suggest such a thing, and I burst into tears, told her I would not be going back in that river that day or any day in the near future, and certainly not without a life-preserver!

As I reflected on this story, and came up with the title "River of Life" for this chapter, I could see God's hand so clearly and powerfully sparing my life and the lives of my friends in spite of our utter stupidity. For us even to CONSIDER climbing into that river was sheer madness; but how many of us wisely stop to consider such things in our lives? Oh, looking at that one pornographic magazine won't hurt, or visiting that one website; or going out and drinking with my friends and then getting behind the wheel of my car will be ok; or just doing a bit of flirting with my married boss won't hurt anything. The list is endless of the "moments of insanity" that daily race across our paths.

King David had one of those when he saw Bathsheba and took her into his bed; we all know the end of that story: pregnancy, betrayal, murder, and then death. Yet God called David a man after His own heart. God is often so gracious when we act out of sheer stupidity and foolishness. What was the key to God still regarding David as a man after His heart?

"Have mercy on me, O God, according to your unfailing love...for I know my transgressions, and my sin is always before me. Against you, you only, have I sinned and done what is evil in your sight...

The sacrifices of God are a broken spirit; a broken and contrite heart, O God, you will not despise." (Psalm 51: 1, 3, 17) David's repentance set him free from his past so that he could walk into his future with the Lord.

I also learned through my river drama first, how limited my perspectives can be and second, how much we need each other in this life. As I clung to the crack in the rock, thinking that this was my way out, my way of salvation from sure drowning in the rapids, my friend could see everything from a very different perspective. From her view, she saw that I was losing strength, but more importantly, that there was a swirling eddy just underneath that rock, and if I didn't push away from the rock, I could have gotten "swallowed" up in that swirling eddy and drowned underneath that rock. I only learned that fact later, and I thanked her profusely for her insistence that I "LET GO!" At the time, it seemed like she was sending me to my death, but in reality, her words, "let go", saved my life. I've become more and more thankful as the years go by for those people in my life who are willing not only to laugh with me, love me and encourage me, but also speak hard words of truth and reality to me, which from my view seem deadly, but which, in the long run, bring life! "Wounds from a friend can be trusted." (Proverbs 27:6a NIV)

Mostly, though, through this entire near-drowning incident, I see Jesus coming to save me! I am not exaggerating when I say I knew I was dying, I was weak, out of air, pretty much hopeless, watching my life pass before my eyes, and I cried out a desperate cry: "Jesus, save me!" Now I'm not saying that Jesus will only come and save you when you are at the end of your rope and on death's door. But a true lesson for me in this river was that Jesus *wants* us to call out to Him; He stands ready to save, ready to enter into our mess, into our desperation and yank us out and bring us back to life. It's our choice whether we will cry out to Jesus or continue to try to save ourselves, which will end in ultimate failure. "For it is by grace you have been saved, through faith—and this is not from yourselves, it is the gift of God—not by works so that no one can boast." (Ephesians 2:8-9 NIV)

Even our third friend, as she was trying desperately to hang onto her inner tube, which was dragging her back into the river, is a glaring example of so many of us. There are things in our lives that we think we so desperately need to hang on to, that if we don't have, we won't be able to survive or go on. We begin to go into panic mode and all the while God is screaming at us, "Let it go!" Only when we do are we able to see how what used to be a good thing (the tube) has turned into something that could harm us in the end. Ask the Lord what "tubes" you are desperately holding onto that are dragging you down. When He shows you, release them to Him and watch the new freedom you will experience as God deals with your tubes and sets you free! "There is a way that seems right to a man, but in the end it leads to death." (Proverbs 14:12 NIV)

Walking Forward

That day, standing up in that river, I was given a new lease on life by my Heavenly Father. I've gained a lot of wisdom, and hopefully, grown in humility as I realize that going into this river called life, I need to be fully equipped. Those kayakers had their "armor" on: helmets (salvation and wisdom), life-preservers (breastplate of righteousness and shield of faith), river-worthy boats (belt of truth – water skirts – which keep the 'lies' out, feet shod properly); they also had each other, also fully equipped and trained (brothers and sisters in the Body of Christ), and oars (sword of the Spirit – the Word of God) to help them maneuver around and push away from those things which could harm them.

No matter what your particular river looks like, and you may be in the middle of it flailing along like I was, cry out to Jesus, in humility and repentance, recognizing your need, "Save me!" I truly believe that every raging 'river' can become a river of life if we allow Him to make it so.

Questions to consider:

1. What are the "worthless" things you are clinging to that you think will either satisfy or save you? List them here and then bring them to the Lord, let them go into His hands, and cling to Jesus alone.

2. Who are the people in your life who are willing to speak truth to you? Who are the people in your life who are convincing you to swim in dangerous waters? Ask the Lord what He says about each of these people.

3. What situations have you gotten yourself in where you need to cry out to Jesus, "Save me!"? Do that now, and allow the Holy Spirit to speak to your heart.

That day, standing up in that river, I was given a new lease on life by my Heavenly Father. I've gained a lot of wisdom, and hopefully, grown in humility as I realize that going into this river called life, I need to be fully equipped. Those kayakers had their "armor" on: helmets (salvation and wisdom), life-preservers (breastplate of righteousness and shield of faith), river-worthy boats (belt of truth – water skirts – which keep the 'lies' out, feet shod properly); they also had each other, also fully equipped and trained (brothers and sisters in the Body of Christ), and oars (sword of the Spirit – the Word of God) to help them maneuver around and push away from those things which could harm them.

No matter what your particular river looks like, and you may be in the middle of it flailing along like I was, cry out to Jesus, in humility and repentance, recognizing your need, "Save me!" I truly believe that every raging 'river' can become a river of life if we allow Him to make it so.

Questions to consider:

1. What are the "worthless" things you are clinging to that you think will either satisfy or save you? List them here and then bring them to the Lord, let them go into His hands, and cling to Jesus alone.

2. Who are the people in your life who are willing to speak truth to you? Who are the people in your life who are convincing you to swim in dangerous waters? Ask the Lord what He says about each of these people.

3. What situations have you gotten yourself in where you need to cry out to Jesus, "Save me!"? Do that now, and allow the Holy Spirit to speak to your heart.

Chapter 4

Trapped in a Stairwell

As I was preparing to leave for school one Friday, I called to my cats Toby and Simon to come in from the enclosed stairwell in the building where I lived and where I regularly let them roam in the mornings. When I had let them into the stairwell that morning, there was an acrid smell of cat urine, which I made a mental note of so I could clean the stairwell in the afternoon after work. Toby came bounding into the house at my whistle, but Simon, my timid boy, was no where to be found. I then looked around my house, and down into the yard outside, thinking he may have somehow "escaped", and I even unlocked my neighbor's door to see if she had let him in her flat before leaving for work. Simon was nowhere to be found. I again stood at the door of the four-story stairwell and whistled. No Simon.

It dawned on me that maybe Simon had found himself a nice place up on the 4th floor landing, where he sometimes liked to hide; but he usually came when summoned, so this was strange. I made the trek up to the 4th floor landing and lo and behold, there was Simon, crouched in the shape of a rounded bread-loaf, staring toward the wall, behind some boxes which obstructed my view of what was on the landing. I promptly scolded Simon, grabbed him, without looking to see what held **his** attention so intently, and walked down the stairs to my flat to lock him in for the day.

As I began to leave again, I thought, "I wonder if the rancid urine smell in the stairwell is from another cat, one of the yard cats who accidentally got locked in the stairwell...and, I wonder if that cat is up on that 4th floor landing behind those boxes!" So, I laid my bags down and trekked back up the stairs; peeking out from behind the boxes was a terrified looking black cat, huddled in the same bread-loaf position Simon had been in. Caution flooded my mind as I put two and two together. I realized that indeed, the acrid urine smell was a result of this cat having been locked in the stairwell, probably all night, and that if Simon, my shy, timid little boy could somehow hold this cat in place, then this cat was scared and who knows what a scared cat will do?

I gently moved a foot toward the cat who promptly growled and hissed at me, and I tried to talk to her in calm tones, to ease her out of her safe haven. In a flash, she scurried from her hiding place and raced past me down the first flight of stairs to the next landing, stopping only to turn and stare at me with beady green eyes. I started down the stairs after her, slowly, knowing she was terrified of me, but thinking all the time, "I wish she knew I was only here to help her and to set her free from this prison!" We proceeded all the way down the flights of stairs this way, her stopping for a short second to turn and stare at this woman who was obviously, from her perspective, trying to hurt her. When we reached the bottom of the stairs where the door leading into the courtyard is, this big black cat scurried in the opposite direction from the door and under the stairs into the dark haven where she probably had urinated. I quickly made my way to the courtyard door and turned around to let her know and to show her she was FREE, only to see her racing back up the stairs, quick as lightning, probably to her 4th floor hiding place.

So, once again, I trekked up the stairs and there she was, huddled between box and wall. She hissed at me again as I tried to coax her from her hiding place. She raced down the stairs again but instead of stopping at the landing, she raced straight ahead and leapt with all her power, slamming her body into the closed window on the 3rd floor landing. At first I wanted to laugh—it was pretty hilarious to see this cat scrambling desperately to get away and claw her way up to the top of the window. However, my laughter was quickly squelched as her fearful desperation dawned on me. She continued to screech and tried to claw her way to the top of the window, only to slide down again. My heart was breaking as her terror filled body stepped back and leapt again at the window, slamming herself against it, trying desperately to break free. When she fell to the ground the second time, she turned and raced down the next flight of stairs. I was nearly in tears at this point, wanting so much to help her, but realizing there was nothing I could do except keep my distance and try to coax her down the stairs to the open door to freedom.

On the 2nd floor landing, she did the same thing, literally throwing her entire body at the window, and hitting it so hard that it nearly broke! She clawed her way desperately to the top of the window and then slid to the ground. By this time, I was miserable, watching this poor cat's desperation unfold before me, knowing she was terrified of me, her liberator, and me, her liberator, completely helpless in communicating to her that freedom is hers for the having, and she no longer has to slam herself against closed windows, trying to set herself free!

Finally, she raced down the last set of stairs, rounded the corner and saw the open door before her and raced out the door to freedom!!! I breathed a HUGE sigh of relief as I watched her stop for a moment in the middle of the yard, then race to the tree, claw her way up the tree and race across the top of the building to freedom!!!

What an ordeal. What a heartbreaking scene to witness. And then it struck me: how much like this cat are so many people without Jesus, without hope. However, even some people who have a relationship with Jesus are like this cat, slamming themselves up against what seem like open ways of escape, but turn out to be closed windows, and they end up bruising themselves as they slam themselves against them and try to claw their way out of situations!

I believe there are a number of different people who can be found in this story; let's have a look at some of them.

There are those people who find themselves feeling completely trapped, and like this cat urinating in the stairwell, start to make complete messes out of their situations, reaching the point of just wanting to survive. They are terrified, and eventually hide themselves away, far from anyone, so as not to be discovered in their dilemma. They don't want help. They've reached a point where they cannot even imagine that there could be a way out.

Then there are those people who feel trapped and are hiding away in a safe place they've found, knowing there will be a chance for escape somehow, but choosing to bide their time until the opportune moment. They are not seeking out help, but staying hidden so as not to be discovered and hopefully, the mess they've gotten themselves in will simply work itself out.

Then there are the people who are discovered hiding. God has come to find them, and once discovered, they look with skeptical eyes at the One who wants, more than anything, to help them out of their situation. They are leery and scared, because what they have heard or experienced of God and/or from His children is judgment, anger, condemnation, and criticism. "Leave me alone!" they say. When gently approached by a loving hand, they run, only looking back to see if God is continuing to pursue them, because if He is, they're going to keep running, keeping a safe distance, so as not to be hurt again.

Walking Forward

We now come to those who have run from God, trying desperately to find a way out, and when the door is opened to them, they don't even notice it. In their fear, they flee back to where they came from as fast as they can go, to their safe hiding place, where they have found their own comfort, even though it is cold, damp, dark and there is no freedom. They heard the voice of God and saw the open door out of the corner of their eye as they were fleeing. However, they believe they know better, and they prefer the safety of their comfort zone, where they feel they are in control, to what God has promised them: true freedom!

The next type of person may even be a Christian; he or she has prayed the prayer of salvation, and may have even walked for many years with God. Yet, a situation comes along where every door seems to be closed, every window locked, and fear kicks in, leading to hopelessness and even despair. These people have led a very controlled Christian life, where things have generally sailed along quite smoothly, but suddenly, something extremely challenging confronts them and they find themselves feeling trapped. The situation smells acrid, rancid, and there seems to be no way out. Along comes God or even one of His children, gently speaking words of encouragement and love, caring deeply for these people, but what God or this child of God has to offer doesn't fit in with what these people have become accustomed to, to "the way God has always worked before." In their frantic desire to maintain control of their lives and try to find a workable solution to their current problem, they flee.

Seeing light and a seemingly good solution, they leap at it, only to slam themselves into a closed window, which indeed is letting in light to the situation, but which does not provide permanent change. They strive and strive, trying to make it work, and finally, out of desperation, turn and run to the next level where, once again, they see what they think is an open window leading to freedom from this situation. They put everything in them into this false solution and again, slam themselves against a closed window. They can see the outside, they can see freedom, they have even tasted that freedom before, but their methods of getting there only end up leaving them bruised and confused.

Finally, we come to those people, who could be any of those discussed above, who finally turn the corner, recognize the open door, which God the Father provided for them through His Son Jesus' death on the cross, and they run free. "Enter by the narrow gate, for wide is the gate and broad is the way that leads to destruction, and there are many who go in by it. Because narrow is the gate and difficult is the way which leads to life and there are few who find it." (Matthew 7:13-14 NKJV) For this cat, and for all of these people, there is One door to freedom, and that is through Jesus Christ. "I am the way and the truth and the life. No one comes to the Father except through me." (John 14:6 NIV)

Someone may say, "But what about those you said were already Christians? They've already gone through the door. What is the door for them?" The door is still Jesus, but walking free is walking in the power of the Holy Spirit, free from the things that can keep us from walking in the fullness of the Holy Spirit. Such things might include hurts from the past, lies from the enemy that we continue to believe, bad habit patterns we've established over the years, addictions, fears, anxieties, worries, even age-old religious traditions or beliefs that we've adhered to so vigilantly that we've slowly adopted conscious or even subconscious beliefs such as "this is how God works," or "this is the way we should do things". The door leads to God's mercies, which are new every morning, and the power of the Holy Spirit, which is not limited by the walls and windows of the stairwell, but is vastly open, like the sky stretching above and the fresh, clean air that completely surrounds us as we step out of our stairwell and into His endless presence!

Most mornings after this incident, as I walked into the stairwell, down the stairs and out the door to the open courtyard, I breathed in the freshness of the Holy Spirit anew. I thank God for setting me free through Jesus' death on the cross, and invite God to put to death and to help me to put to death any preconceived fleshly notions of how I believe He should work in and through me. Instead, I ask Him to pour into me His Holy Spirit to change me permanently and work through me in the ways that HE knows are the very best for me and for His glory.

"For I know the plans I have for you declares the Lord, plans to prosper you and not to harm you, plans to give you a hope and a future. Then you will call upon me and come and pray to me, and I will listen to you. You will seek me and find me when you seek me with all your heart. I will be found by you, declares the Lord, and will bring you back from captivity." (Jeremiah 29:11-14a NIV)

The New King James Version reads: "For I know the thoughts that I think towards you, says the Lord, thoughts of peace and not of evil, to give you a future and a hope. Then you will call upon me and go and pray to me and I will listen to you. And you will seek me and find me when you search for me with all your heart. I will be found by you and I will bring you back from your captivity." (Jeremiah 29:11-14a)

For every one of the people discussed above, these verses in Jeremiah are true, from the one who has never even heard the name of Jesus to the one who has walked with God for years. God is in the business of bringing people <u>out</u> of captivity and into His grace-based freedom! God's Truth never fails and we can stand on the Truth that, "It is for freedom that Christ has set us free. Stand firm then and do not let yourselves be burdened again by a yoke of slavery." (Galatians 5:1 NIV)

Finally, let us not lose heart, as the cat in the stairwell seemed to do, but rather let us rest on the truth spoken in 2 Corinthians 3:17: "Now the Lord is the Spirit, and where the Spirit of the Lord is, there is freedom." (NIV)

Questions to consider:

1. Do you find yourself relating to any of the "people" described in this chapter? If so, who, and what does your experience "in the stairwell" look like?

2. What truths from the Word of God have you either forgotten or not believed, and what has the result been?

3. List the promises of God which the Holy Spirit brought to your heart and mind as you read this chapter. Meditate on His promises, His truths, this week.

Chapter 5

Locked Doors

We had parent/teacher conferences at school one evening. In our school in Hungary, all teachers are assigned a room in which to be for conferences (we don't have our own classrooms), and parents look at the list of names and rooms to determine where they need to go to find their child's teachers.

I arrived to find I was to be in room 126 with one other teacher. Parents were mingling around, and I looked for the key. There was no key to be found in the school, so, the door remained locked and the room darkened. The other teacher who was supposed to be there had found another room, displaced the teachers who were supposed to be in there, and proceeded with her conferences. I decided to plant myself on the bench outside the darkened classroom and as parents came to inquire, I was there. I found myself becoming a silent observer.

I watched as parents arrived, walked up to the door, tried the handle, and saw it was locked and the room was dark. Yet some of them stood there, continuing to wait. It seemed to me that they thought that maybe somehow, miraculously, the door would open...or something. Others tried two or three times, looked around, and walked off. Others asked those standing nearby if they knew anything about the teachers who were supposed to be in that room. Since none of them was asking for me, I remained silent, not knowing where to point them to find the other teacher who was supposed to be in that classroom.

There were, and are, many reactions to closed, locked doors and darkened rooms. "But they are supposed to be here!" "You can't change things on me, I cannot handle that change!" "But the sheet SAYS room 126, so I'm going to wait here!"

The teachers were still available, just in different places...they had not changed; they remained the same...but it took some openness on the parents' parts to realize that maybe they had to do something "out of the ordinary" or something "they were not used to doing" in order to meet the teachers. They may have had to shift their paradigm to see things from a different perspective, to experience things in a new way. Of course they could still meet with the "unchanged" teachers...but for some, I could readily see that it was VERY uncomfortable to have to "change" locations.

Interestingly, and not necessarily surprisingly, I think that some followers of Jesus become uncomfortable when God shows up in a different place or even in a different way than we are accustomed to.

He's not changed, but He's drawing us to Himself, the unchanging God, in a new location, and we may have to change our thinking about how "things are supposed to be" with Him. I'm not talking about a geographical change, but a paradigm shift. God is in the business of taking us to new places in Himself, and He sometimes, or often, if we are open to it, does that by making us a bit uncomfortable. He does not want us standing at the locked door, stuck in the ways in which we are comfortable functioning. Rather, He wants us to seek Him with all our heart, mind, soul and strength, and that may mean going to uncomfortable, unfamiliar places in His Holy Spirit. In fact, walking in increasing freedom in Christ is inevitably going to mean change. Our nicely predictable and controlled environments are often radically transformed, and we don't always like that, because feeling some semblance of control is quite comforting and pleasant.

If you examine the Gospels where Jesus heals various blind people, He never does it the same way twice. Also, when he heals various illnesses or drives out demons from people, each time it is different. All of these people's lives were changed, and most likely had to continue to change as a result of having encountered Jesus. I believe that true freedom in Jesus is allowing Him to be God, and realizing that even though He never changes, what He does and how He does it very well could change. But His changes will always bring us greater freedom and intimacy in our relationship with Him as every day is fresh, new and exciting! The blind could see, the lame could walk, the demonized were set free—new lives unfolded! We should expect to see that today as well, but we have to rid ourselves of our 'locked door' mentalities!

God does not necessarily ask us to understand; He always asks us to trust Him. "Trust in the Lord with all your heart and lean not on your own understanding; In all your ways acknowledge him, and he will make your paths straight. (Proverbs 3:5-6 NIV) If we always understood, then we would not have to have faith in Him. We could have faith in our understanding, and to have faith in anything but Him alone can easily lead to idolatry.

Lord, help us to see that locked doors may mean new freedoms are emerging, and we simply need to seek You in that new place!

Questions to consider:

1. What are some of the "locked doors" you have encountered and how have you responded to them?

2. Are there any places in your own heart where you have put limits on how God can work in your life or in other people's lives? Take time to ask God to show you where you need to ask for His forgiveness.

Chapter 6

Freedom In Stillness

"Be still, and know that I am God..." (Psalm 46:10 NKJV)

Our boots were soaked to the point of making squishing sounds with each step. After two days of walking in heavy, water-logged boots, my friend and I were thrilled to open the bathroom door in our hotel room and see those electric drying "pipes" on which you can hang clothing or towels, crank up the heat and they'll dry in record time!

"Well," we both thought, "why not slide our boots onto these pipes and let them dry from the inside out?"

Has God ever turned up the heat on you on the inside? Have you, like our boots, just had to stay exactly where you were placed by God and simply be still and allow the heat of His purifying fire burn away that which does not belong inside of you?

It's often in these times when the heat is cranked up on the INSIDE that the last thing we want to do is be still. We want relief and we want it now! God's fire serves three purposes: purification, destruction of sin, and igniting for ministering the Gospel. But it is only when we get still that His fire can do its work in us and through us!

Now, we could have set the boots *near* the pipes, or we could have simply *hoped* they would dry by morning and set them out on the balcony in the fresh air. We humans have all kinds of ways that we think will bring healing and wholeness to our lives, don't we? If we 'do less of this' or 'do more of that' then healing will come and more freedom in our relationship with God will unfold. However, when it doesn't work, we wonder why, and we keep going around the same mountain again and again, and all the while, God is calling us to be still before Him, let his purifying heat do its work, and know that He is God.

First, it goes against our very nature to 'be still'. Time and again we've heard it said we are human 'beings' not human 'doings', yet we continue to think that 'doing' will bring change. Mary knew what to 'do' — she "sat at the Lord's feet listening to what he said." (Luke 10:39 NIV) Jesus commended her for her stillness. She wanted to *know* her Savior, to hear His voice; and being still before Him is one of the truest and deepest ways we can *know* our God and hear His voice.

Our boots hung on the heated pipes and we had to keep a close eye on them so that nothing happened to them that would harm them.

God does the same with us when we are in the fire of His purifying love. He keeps His gracious eye on us, and as we remain still and know that He is God and ruthlessly trust that all He does is out of His great love for us, we are made pure and fully whole in the ways He has intended for us. We are ultimately set free by remaining still in His presence. That which has slogged us down, made us heavy and may have even brought pain through "blisters" is removed in His loving embrace as we remain still.

"Be still before the Lord and wait patiently for Him." (Psalm 37:7 NIV)

I regularly went into the bathroom to look at the boots. From the outside, I couldn't see any change; they looked just like they did when we slipped them on the pipes. However, when I got closer and actually reached out and touched the fabric of the boots, I could feel them becoming increasingly dry. Being patient while the pipes did their job was the key; we too need to be patient with ourselves, and even with others, as God does His work in our lives and in others' lives.

His timing is perfect, His healing is perfect, His purifying heat is perfect, even though it may not FEEL that way; and all lead to perfect freedom to be all that we were created to be, His beloved, healthy, fully functional children. We simply need to be still, trust and know that He is the great I AM. He will remove us from His purifying fire at the perfect time—not a second too early or too late.

"'For I know the plans I have for you,' declares the Lord, 'plans to prosper you and not to harm you, plans to give you hope and a future.'" (Jeremiah 29:11 NIV)

The joy and goodness of having light-weight, dry boots the next day was a blessing beyond words; similarly, we too are blessed and can be a blessing to others as we remain still, listen to His voice, and allow Daddy to heal us, remove the heaviness and set us free!

Questions to consider:

1. What are some things which have "slogged" you down in your relationship with the Lord?

2. What keeps you from sitting still in the presence of the Lord? Ask the Lord to show you His perspective on those things.

Chapter 7

Freedom Road

"A man's heart plans his way, but the Lord directs his steps." (Proverbs 16:9 NKJV)

A cloudless, blue sky welcomed us to Lienz, Austria the morning after our late arrival by train the previous night. We were excited to do some exploring in the city and possible hiking, so we set off to the tourist office.

We decided to hike to the Dolomiten Hut, which, we were told, was now closed for the winter (it was early October), but which could be reached in a day-hike. My friend, Marsha, and I were definitely game and set off in tennis shoes, with jackets, water and snacks for the day. Walking through the village to the start of the trail was pleasant and dry, and sunny skies above promised a wonderful day of mountainous exploration.

As we started up the mountainside, full of lush greenery, we began to hit switch-backs on the road-like trail we were following. Eventually, we began to see snow; and soon we were walking through the packed snow. We'd been warned about sudden storms arising, and that we should watch the sky carefully and turn back if grey clouds began rolling in. However, the sun was still shining with only light, white clouds gently gracing the crystal blue sky above.

In a short time, we were walking through a foot of snow, and the hours of the day were slipping away. "How far was this hut?" we both wondered. Being logical in our endeavors, we noticed that there were electrical wires going straight up the hill, which we, doing our switchbacks crossed under time and time again. Finally, as the clouds began to roll in more thickly, and the snow was getting deeper, I made the suggestion that we leave the path we were following and trek boldly straight up the side of the mountain, following the wires above, which were surely going to the hut. This would definitely save us time!

So, there we were, in our tennis shoes, trudging up the side of a mountain through now knee-deep snow and getting deeper, watching more clouds roll across the sky above, breathing heavily at the extra exertion this pathless route was requiring, and wondering, "Was this such a great idea?" We continued on for probably an hour like this, believing that indeed we were cutting off hours and miles by going off the beaten path. Finally, after getting stuck in the snow and barely able to lift our legs out of the hip-deep snow, we both collapsed and lay back, laughing at our stupidity and trying to catch our breath. Suddenly, I heard something very quiet, but very familiar. Could it be? No! But it was.

Walking Forward

It was the sound of a car engine, and it was not far away! A car meant a road, which meant a much easier route. We both looked in the direction of this all-too familiar noise and there was a car, driving up the snow-packed road not 100 yards from where we sat, sweating, exhausted, and nearly ready to quit. So, we did what any sane women would do, we dug ourselves out of our self-made traps, walked over to the road and proceeded up the mountain to our destination on a well-packed, well-traveled road.

By this time, we were both really tired, and when we arrived at the place where our electrical wires seemed to end, at a small building which was not the Dolomiten Hut, I told Marsha, "I'm done; I'm too tired to go on." She responded, "Ok, but I'm just going to walk up around this corner and see if there is anything there." I happily let her go, sat down, watching the grey clouds roll in, and began dreaming about a hot bath and a large dinner back at our hotel.

Suddenly, I heard Marsha yelling, "Arden, get over here! You are not going to believe this!" Reluctantly, I arose and started walking up the road, around the corner, saying under my breath, "This had better be worth it!" As I rounded the final curve, there was the Dolomiten Hut, but more importantly, rising before us was the most incredible view of the Dolomite Mountains! Breathtaking does not even begin to describe the exquisite beauty of these jagged peaks, stretching as far as the eye could see, covered with snow, and reaching down into the green valley below. I was more than awestruck, and both Marsha and I declared at almost the same time, "This was TOTALLY worth it!!!"

We drank in the view, unable to put into words the incredible landscape lying before us. We ate the rest of our snacks and drank the last of our water, took many pictures, and just relished the magnificent beauty of that place at that moment. It felt like we were living in a postcard!

Neither of us wanted to leave, but the daylight was waning, and we needed to walk down the mountain, even though we'd be taking the "easy" route, following the road. Reluctantly, we turned our backs on the most breathtaking scene either of us had witnessed in our lives, and began the long trek home.

It didn't take long for the Lord to show me many lessons through this adventuresome experience. We truly were ill-equipped for hiking that day, not knowing that snow lay ahead and that tennis shoes would not be sufficient at the higher elevations where winter snows had already fallen not just in inches, but feet! The spiritual question facing each of us is this: are we aware of the journey we are facing, and are we well-equipped? Have I put on the full armor of God to face what lies ahead? Are my feet shod with the Gospel of Peace or with simple tennis shoes…do we really understand we are in a battle and not a game? (Ephesians 6:11-17 NKJV)

The Lord often takes us on paths and trails in our lives that, from our perspective, seem to take forever to walk. There are countless switchbacks and the way appears to be long and tiring. He marks the path well, even when the "weather" changes with the seasons, but am I too impatient to get to my destination and instead start looking for a shorter way? God does not take short-cuts, and when we begin to reason with our fleshly minds and be "logical", we can short-circuit what the Lord is doing and it always leads to difficulty and challenges we were never intended to face. Of course He will let us go that route, and when we finally find ourselves hip-deep in snow, soaking wet, exhausted, frustrated, and ready to quit, He is still right there showing us His way out.

"No temptation has seized you except what is common to man. And God is faithful; he will not let you be tempted beyond what you can bear. But when you are tempted, he will also provide a way out so that you can stand up under it." (1 Corinthians 10:13 NIV)

What we think will be quicker and easier actually turns out to be more detrimental. It could be a temptation to short-circuit what God is doing, or simply our own fleshly desires. If we would obey the Word of God and recognize this truth: "I know, O Lord, that a man's life is not his own; it is not for man to direct his steps," (Jeremiah 10:23 NIV) we would walk in more freedom with the Lord!

We could have continued on in our stubbornness and pride, trekking straight up the side of the mountain through the snow, and we may have eventually reached the top, but in humility, with the small still voice, the almost whispering of the car engine, we recognized God pointing out a better way, His way, along which we could walk quite easily. "You will show me the path of life." (Psalms 16:11 NKJV)

Often we feel ready to give up just before our breakthrough; we feel we just can't go on. We reached the "top", and it's nice and it was a great experience getting there, but pushing any further is just too difficult. Pressing in to God's heart seems to be just too challenging. That's when the Body of Christ is so very essential. Of course, the Holy Spirit can and does prompt and encourage us to keep going; but when discouragement has overtaken someone, God may choose to use another member of the Body to push us to go just a little bit further, just around the corner, to see what the Lord wants to reveal. I was literally 100 yards from the goal, from our final destination, from the blessing, and I nearly gave up. Actually, I had given up, but Marsha kept pressing in and pushing forward. Are we there for someone who needs us to help them press in and push forward?

She could not come and carry me those last 100 yards, just as we cannot walk someone else's walk with God, but she did cry out that the final goal is worth it! Her words of encouragement to "come and see!" were enough to motivate me to push through my exhaustion and frustration, to walk the last 100 yards and receive the blessing!

I remember thinking, "I nearly missed out!" How many of us nearly miss out or literally DO miss out on the blessings God has for us because we "give up" when it gets too hard, or we feel frustrated, or we're just not willing to finish? "You're not going to believe this!" Marsha had cried. Do we really believe that God wants to work in and through our difficult situation and bring us through to His blessings?

Maybe it's a job situation that is taxing you. Maybe it is a relationship that would be easier just to walk away from than go around the corner together, 100 more yards, and receive God's blessings in abundance upon it. The list is endless and you have your own scenario.

Most importantly, the final blessing of heaven awaits those who know Jesus Christ as personal Savior and Lord of their lives. Are we going to "give up" just 100 yards from the end, not really believing the Word which declares that glorious experiences with Him and eventually, eternity with Him, awaits us, and both are beyond our wildest dreams or imaginations?

"I run in the path of Your commands, for You have set my heart free." (Psalm 119:32 NIV)

God's glory was revealed through that incredible view of the Dolomite Mountains; it will be His glory revealed in the end as well!

I pray that these lessons from this road to freedom will encourage you in whatever situation you find yourself in, to look to our loving, patient, Heavenly Father, who longs to guide, lead and bless each one of us with more than we could ever ask or imagine! As we move into Part II: Experiencing Freedom and Forgiveness, may the Holy Spirit guide us into all Truth and set us free to experience more of Him.

"Now to him who is able to do immeasurably more than all we ask or imagine, according to his power that is at work within us, to him be glory in the church and in Christ Jesus throughout all generations, for ever and ever! Amen." (Ephesians 3:20-21 NIV)

Questions to consider:

1. What paths have you taken off and away from God's path, and where have these led you?

2. In what ways have you been a "Marsha" to a friend in the Body of Christ and encouraged that friend to keep pressing in to Jesus? Who has been a "Marsha" to you? Take a minute to thank God for those people in your life.

Part II

Experiencing Freedom and Forgiveness

Chapter 8

Collars for Healing

When my cat Simon was ten years old, he had a small growth on his leg which the vet said needed to be removed through surgery and sent off to pathology to determine if it was cancerous or not. So, Simon was put to sleep, and the surgery went well; when he woke up, he had a plastic, cone-shaped, hood-like collar tied around his neck with white gauze, to keep him from licking the surgical spot. Simon would have to wear the collar for ten days, and it was obvious from the start, he was not happy about it, and it was a very disturbing situation for him.

When I got him home, he was still coming out of the anesthesia and would have these spurts of running come over him; unfortunately, he would run very close to the edge of the doorway and slam into it with the plastic collar. This would stop him, and he would slowly back up, sit down and look very dazed and confused. He would get up again and try walking forward, but again, cutting too close to the door-jam and he'd hit the plastic collar against it. It took only two hours of this running, slamming, backing up and hitting the plastic collar against doorways for the collar to split apart. So off we were again to the vet to get a new collar!

This time when we got home, and as Simon would approach a doorway, I would try to guide him toward the center of the doorway, so the collar would not impede his progress. Then he would hang his head low and the collar would catch on the rug or floor, paralyzing him in that position until he figured out he needed to lift his head, or until I came over and gently lifted his head. Of course Simon tried to do everything to remove this annoying collar—he shook his head violently, or tried to pull it off using his paws. Watching him try to clean himself was just a pitiful sight as he would lick and lick and not really realize he was simply licking the inside of the plastic cone-like collar. As frustrating as it must have been for him, it was also difficult for me to watch him struggle and know that he did not understand this new situation.

In a matter of moments, Simon, who had no idea anything was wrong with him, went to the vet, was put to sleep, woke up and his entire world was a different place. The collar was obviously extremely uncomfortable, but very necessary, and for his good; but he certainly couldn't understand that, nor was I able to explain it to him, no matter how many soothing words I used or reassuring strokes I gave him. His surgical wound needed to heal, and this was the only solution. He was unable to do some things for himself, and he had to change the way he did other things, like eating and drinking. He could no longer go out the cat-door, nor was he allowed to go downstairs and into the yard. The frustration of the learning process was obvious as I could literally see him become increasingly timid and almost depressed. He would look with longing at Toby, my other cat and his buddy, who was free to roam all day long in the yard. Everything within me longed to have him understand that this was necessary, this was for his good, for his healing, and that it would indeed only be for a season. I found myself spending more time petting him and just being with him, loving on him more than I ever had before.

I could so much relate to Simon and the collar in a season of this exciting journey I am on with the Lord. I knew this time was simply a season, and it was painful for me, but I too had to be patient and persevering. It was as though the Lord had put a large, plastic conical collar around my neck as well, and I had to learn how to do many things completely differently. I found myself slamming into door-jams, walking with my head bowed and missing out on the things right in front of me; I moved more slowly, with more caution; there were times when I tried to do things in the "old" ways, but I've learned to accept the new ways of functioning. I know in my heart that these new ways are better and healthier ways, but the process of unlearning old habits is difficult and sometimes painful. As the adage goes: old habits die hard!

When Simon stayed close to the wall, he hit the edge of the doorways and had to stop. He had to back up and move closer to the middle of the open doorway, where he could walk through easily. So too, God broke me out of my comfort zone and forced me to move along another path, which is actually more open and free, but it means greater risk, and nothing to lean on or cling to anymore; instead it means complete trust in Him alone. "Trust in the Lord with all your heart and lean not on your own understanding. In all your ways acknowledge Him and He will direct your paths." (Proverbs 3:5-6 NKJV)

The collar was necessary on Simon in order to let the wound heal. My neighbor wanted to take it off a couple of days early as she felt so sorry for Simon. However, for complete healing of our wounds to occur, *everyone* must let it heal properly, and no one can step in to try to "fix it" in another way. Only when God is allowed to do the healing will the process and timing of healing be perfect.

Simon had a growth on his leg. The growth shouldn't have been there; we don't know how he got it or what it was. Often in life, our situation is not the way it "should be". Maybe it's the result of a wound or maybe a poor choice—regardless, it is what it is, and it must be dealt with by God for there to be healing and growth. It would have been "death" to Simon if I had simply left him with the wound without keeping him "collared in" and protected, or if I had left him to figure out how to do everything himself 100%. God's divine interventions in our times of need, when we are wounded or in the healing process are life-giving to us.

Sometimes, we do need the body of Christ, and unfortunately, there are times in the Church when either we leave the wounded lying on the side of the road, bleeding and hurting, or when they are in the healing process, we jump ship and leave. What we need is God's wisdom in every situation to know how we can be the part of the body of Christ to those in the process of healing, allowing God to put the collars on and set the boundaries and complete His healing while doing what He directs us to do to aid in that situation.

Jumping ship and cutting ties is easy in the short-run and very selfish. Bearing with one another and loving our brothers and sisters as Christ loves us is the constant, daily challenge which is costly, but worth it in the long run. "We then who are strong ought to bear with the scruples of the weak and not to please ourselves." (Romans 15:1 NKJV)

I couldn't wait for day ten to arrive so that I could finally remove the collar from Simon's neck. The night before, as he lay quietly at the foot of my bed, staring at me pitifully, I spoke to him saying, "Tomorrow morning you will be free from that silly collar!" Of course he didn't understand, and he was pleasantly surprised when I cut it off of him the next morning. This picture makes me wonder how excited God must be when He knows we're ready to have certain collars removed so that we can run free again, having learned the lessons we needed to learn and having been transformed according to His Truth!

Simon has changed; he seems calmer, he now walks through the center of the doorway, and he's a bit more loving and approachable. Maybe he'll eventually go back to his old ways, but maybe the positive changes will remain. When God puts collars on us, and takes us through uncomfortable times, asking us to change because He knows it is for our ultimate good and healing, are we willing to endure the season, or do we continue to slam into the walls, doorways, floors and stubbornly insist on doing it our way rather than God's way? Lord, help us to see that the transformations and healings that You bring are for our ultimate good and Your glory!

"You are good, and what you do is good; teach me your decrees." (Psalm 119:68 NIV)

From eternity, God saw, chose and invested in us; are we as His chosen children willing, when called upon, to see, accept, love and invest in those He brings into our lives for this relatively brief period we know as a lifetime? Are we willing to be His instruments of grace and mercy that in the end, our brothers and sisters will experience increased freedom in Jesus?

"Let us not become weary in doing good, for at the proper time we will reap a harvest if we do not give up. Therefore, as we have opportunity, let us do good to all people, especially to those who belong to the family of believers." (Galatians 6:9-10 NIV)

Questions to consider:

1. Has the Lord ever put a "collar" on you for a season? If so, what was that collar-experience like,

and what are the specific lessons that you learned during that time?

2. In what ways have others either "jumped ship" or come alongside you during a season when you were going through God's healing process? Have you forgiven those who chose not to stand with you during that time? If you have not, take time right now to forgive and release those individuals into the hands of the Father!

Chapter 9

Log-Jams to Freedom

I coached the varsity girls' soccer team at a private Christian day-school in Charlottesville, Virginia for six years. One of our "duties" as coaches was to drive the buses on which the teams traveled to both home and away games. We drove those big yellow school buses, which we painted blue and white (our school colors), and while very challenging, they were also quite fun to drive.

It was our last game of my last season as coach, and we were in Richmond, Virginia playing against our biggest rival, Collegiate. Only once in six years had we beaten this team, and unfortunately, on this day, we lost in the league championship. Our varsity girls' lacrosse team had also lost their championship game in Richmond, and both teams, with both buses, ended up at one of the local Burger Kings for dinner before heading back up Interstate 64 home to Charlottesville. As I and the field hockey teams' coach commiserated over our losses (this was the last coaching season for both of us), we came up with a fun idea to end the season on a high note. We would have a bus race home!

As we lumbered along Interstate 64, which is a median divided highway with two lanes in each direction, I was in the lead. Now you must understand that these buses have something on them called a governor, which is a device in the engine prohibiting the bus from going over a certain speed limit. Well, my co-coaches' buses' governor was set just about ½ mile per hour faster than ours I believe, and so she pulled up alongside our bus and was slowly edging ahead when we came to a hill. My bus functioned much better on the downhill, so I would close the gap and even pull ahead every time we came to those sections of road.

However, our two buses remained side-by-side on this two-lane interstate. Neither one of us wanted to give way to the other, so we simply continued jockeying for position, with each of our teams cheering us on not to give in to the other. For the other coach and me, it was simple fun...at first. Then stubbornness and pride began kicking in. This was our last game, our last trip in these buses, our last chance to prove ourselves.

I looked in my side-view mirror and noticed cars beginning to line up in both lanes directly behind our buses. With the speed limit at 65 mph. on this section of the highway, we, in our governor regulated buses, were only able to hit a maximum of between 55 and 60 mph. It did not take long for a long line of very angry drivers to line up behind our buses. I was in the right lane and my friend was in the left lane, so naturally, I assumed she would do the "right thing" and slow down and pull in behind me so that cars could pass both of us.

However, she remained stubborn and proud, as did I, both of us pressing the gas pedal to the floor. After about ten minutes, there were probably 10-20 cars stretched out behind us in both lanes, honking horns, flashing lights, and expressing their frustration and anger with us.

I finally relented and began slowing down, much to the chagrin of my team who yelled at me from the back of the bus, "We can't let them win!" My friend pulled in front of us and over to the right-hand lane and the log-jam of cars behind us began to unravel and be released. People were honking their horns, giving rude hand gestures and yelling expletives out their windows. I realized that the name of our Christian school was plastered across the sides of both buses...not a great testimony. As the cars continued to race past us, the log-jam behind us was released and the free-flow of traffic on the interstate resumed.

As I reflected on this fun and funny incident, God uncovered His truths. What started out as healthy fun, deteriorated when stubbornness, competition and pride kicked in; cars began getting stuck behind us, just like the free flow of God's Spirit can be hindered in our lives. As prideful determination melded into "I've got to win, to get ahead, to be in control, no matter what the cost," freedom was squelched completely and a full-blown log-jam, stretching as far back as we could see, resulted. The Bible says that "God resists the proud but gives grace to the humble." (James 4:6 NKJV) Our pride led to anger, bitterness and frustration in the hearts of many people who were stuck in the log-jam behind our two buses. I believe that often, when we are blinded by our stubbornness or pride, we don't even see the impact that pride has on not only us, but those around us and even beyond. Proverbs 16:5 paints an even more startling picture of how God views pride. "Everyone proud in heart is an abomination to the Lord." (NKJV) Ouch!

The only thing that freed up the log-jam was humility, and it will always be humility that will free up the Holy Spirit's flow in our lives. We live in freedom solely because of God's grace and He freely pours out that grace to those who are humble.

As the drivers passed by and expressed their discontent, frustration, anger and bitterness, and I waved and mouthed "I'm sorry" to them, I understood to a greater degree how, even when we humble ourselves before God, all the junk that has been built up inside of us as a result of pride must still be released and nailed to the cross of Jesus Christ. The junk doesn't simply disappear; sometimes habits have taken root in us and need to be removed, and at times that can take time. Again, God gives His grace to us as the mucky flow of what bound us comes pouring out to be released into the healing blood of Jesus. Only with release can freedom in the Holy Spirit flow unhindered.

Where in your life are stubbornness and/or pride creating a log-jam? Is it in your marriage? A friendship? At your workplace with a colleague? Maybe you don't even realize there is a log-jam, but you wonder why the free flow of the Holy Spirit is not what it used to be or should be in your life. Ask the Lord to show you any pride or stubbornness in you and in any of your relationships; if He shows you that indeed, you have created a log-jam, repentance in humility is your key to freedom through His grace!

Questions to consider:

1. If there is a log-jam in your relationship with God or with others, what is keeping you from confessing that, repenting and receiving God's forgiveness and freedom?

2. What are some of the fruits of pride? What are the fruits of humility? (You may want to find verses from the Scriptures.)

Chapter 10

Freedom Through Surgery

"Arden's arches are falling down, falling down, falling down!" my surgeon sang as he came into the operating room. In my semi-drugged stupor, I had to laugh. As I lay there preparing to undergo "exploratory" surgery on my foot, I thought about how wonderful it would be to be free of pain, finally, after having limped around in constant pain for nearly a year.

Every day I would awaken, put weight on my foot and the dull pain would start, often intensifying and becoming sharp, but never truly leaving, unless I simply lay down, and then it would become a dull ache. X-rays had revealed nothing; physical therapy had not helped; rest had not brought relief. So here we were at the "last" step: surgery.

For so long in my walk with Jesus, I clung to the belief that more Bible study, more prayer, more Scripture memorization, getting involved in more Christian activity would be the ticket to healing and freedom from the pain, hurt, lostness, loneliness and struggles I often felt. Of course all of these things are important, just like the various methods my doctor and I had tried to bring healing to my foot. In fact, these disciplines—in both realms——do and did some good. After physical therapy and rest, I could sometimes go for hours at a time and feel no pain in my foot; memorizing verses is excellent as it plants God's Word in our hearts where it will remain.

However, when Christian activities are done outside of the context of a deep, intimate, loving soul and Spirit-searching relationship with a loving and good God, they become religious activities which can, like the physical therapy and rest for my foot, only give temporary relief, while the much deeper issues remain untouched.

It wasn't until the surgeon took his knife and opened up my foot that the root of my problem emerged. I had suffered a cracked bone in the arch of my foot that no x-ray had picked up on. My doctor proceeded to shave down that bone—the necessary procedure for complete healing. That surgeon knew what was best and what would bring complete healing.

Anyone who has undergone surgery and been under anesthesia probably knows that moment of slight panic that hits when you realize maybe you won't wake up after the surgery. You are in the hands of the medical professionals and their expertise; it takes tremendous courage to say "yes" to the surgeon, sign the release papers and place your trust in him or her.

In the same way, when more Bible study, more Christian activity, more church involvement isn't working to heal the brokenness inside, it takes tremendous courage to sign the release papers on our life and allow the Great Surgeon and His knife to enter in and cut us open and show us the cracked parts within that are the source of our pain. Yet, when we sign, and when He reveals the root of the lies we have believed based on the wounding we have endured, our task then becomes to bring it all to the cross—the pain, the brokenness, the judgments, everything—leave it at the cross, and receive His healing, freeing, cleansing blood of forgiveness!

I truly thought that after the surgery, I would awaken and while I would have discomfort, I would feel much better. However, when I awoke in the recovery room, such excruciating pain coursed through my entire body that I literally screamed and yelled. They'd put a plaster cast on my foot and my foot had swelled up inside the cast. As a result, the surgical wound was pressing hard against the inside of the cast and it literally felt like a knife being driven into the inside arch of my foot. On top of that, I was freezing cold and my blood pressure began to skyrocket. I was worse off, I felt, than before I went into surgery. Nurses rushed around placing warm blankets on me, trying to explain that they couldn't give me any more pain medication just yet. Tears flowed and I yelled loudly as my throbbing foot continued to send shooting pains throughout my body. I begged them to cut the cast off, telling them it was too tight, but they ignored my pleas.

How often, when we allow God to open up a deeply wounded place in us, knowing that He is coming in to bring healing, do we end up going through a dark season of sometimes excruciating pain, where healing and recovery seem to be more painful than the initial problem?

"But wait, God! I thought You loved me? I thought your healing meant something different than this!?" It sometimes appears we're worse off than before His surgery. But God's ways are higher than our ways. "'For my thoughts are not your thoughts, neither are your ways my ways,' declares the Lord. 'As the heavens are higher than the earth, so are my ways higher than your ways and my thoughts than your thoughts.'" (Isaiah 55:8-9 NIV)

Those nurses could have "aborted" their responsibilities and cut the cast off my foot to bring me relief—but they didn't. Have you ever aborted the process God has you in for your healing? Have you ever, because you were suffering even more than before you initially cried out to God for healing, begged to be relieved of the pain when God, in His great love and mercy was doing a deep, deep healing in you with the ultimate goal of setting you free to walk without a limp? We abort in many ways: we may run to our false comforts like food or watching more TV, getting busier—anything to numb the pain and in the process, run from God. Aborting can also be seen in engaging in more Christian activity; that too can be simply numbing the pain in a "Christian" way.

I spent two hours in the recovery room, then two more days in the hospital and then six weeks in that cast. Healing and freedom is a process and when God does it, he does it perfectly, allowing all the necessary steps, even the painful ones, so that we will no longer be crippled children.

I wish I could say that I lay in that recovery room and cried out to God alone—instead, I cried out to humans to relieve my pain. Oh, I'm sure in those cries I also cried out to God, but I know I was looking primarily to the nurses and doctors—to people—to bring relief. Indeed God can and will use his people in our lives as His instruments, but they can never become our Source or the place we run to first.

The Psalmist, David, knew where to run: "The Lord is my rock and my fortress and my deliverer; My God, my strength in whom I will trust; My shield and the horn of my salvation, my stronghold." (Psalm 18:2 NKJV)

God is the Alpha and the Omega, the beginning and the end. He is intimately acquainted with every "cracked bone" inside of us—and He longs to heal us fully and completely and set us free! Let us run to Him first, last and in between and allow Him to provide for and heal us perfectly and set us free in His way, in His time, through His perfect love.

Questions to consider:

1. What "surgery" is the Lord wanting to do in your heart during this season? What fears, if any, do you have regarding this 'surgery'?

2. What are some verses from Scripture that have been an encouragement to you as you have gone through the Lord's 'surgeries' in your life?

Chapter 11

Freedom's Sometimes Painful Limits

Nothing was more fun for me as a young skier than to spend days with other very good skiers, on excellent slopes in Colorado, traversing intermediate and advanced slopes, laughing and challenging each others' skills.

It was day four, the last of our wonderful holiday, about 10 o'clock in the morning, and twelve of us were jetting down the mountain playing follow the leader. We arrived at an advanced slope which ran under one of the chairlifts at this particular ski area, and the section directly under the lift was riddled with large bumps, always a temptation for skilled skiers. After three days of hard skiing, my lower back was pretty wrecked and tired, so when we headed toward the moguls, I hesitated, but decided to give it a shot since it was our last day of skiing.

After about two moguls, I realized my back was hurting badly and sending me warning signals. I quickly thought, "Well, if I just sort of 'glide' over the mogul, instead of jumping from one to the next, I should be ok." So, as I glided over the top of one mogul, my ski tips firmly planted themselves into the next mogul below like poles driven into concrete. Of course I was flung head over skis, face-first toward the snow, both bindings releasing my boots from the skis, and arms outstretched in front of me to try to catch my fall. I had those molded grip strap poles which do not release, and as I plowed hands and face-first into the snow, directly under the lift, hat, goggles and pride were all strewn across the slope. I could hear the audible gasps from the lift above, but when I declared that I was "ok", clapping erupted from every chair above me along with shouts of "9.5" and "10"!

I struggled to my feet and began the trek back up the mountain to collect my skis, and it was only when I reached for the first ski and tried to pick it up that I realized my left thumb no longer functioned properly. Shooting pain, all the way up my arm let me know that I'd done some major damage. Finally, I was able to use my right hand and the functioning fingers on my left to get myself back in my skis and make my way down to where our group was standing about 50 meters down the mountain, waiting for me. I was gripping both ski poles in my right hand and letting my left arm dangle at my side. Thankfully, we just happened to be skiing with an orthopedic surgeon.

"Dr. Waldron, I think I just broke my thumb!" He carefully pulled off my glove and gently pulled my thumb sideways and backwards toward my wrist. My thumb bent all the way back and touched my forearm, much to the fascination of my doctor who said he usually sees these injuries, called a games-keeper's thumb, the day after when they are too stiff to move this easily. I nearly lost my breakfast right there on the mountain side as he continued to examine my freely dangling thumb and giving instructions as to what I needed to do in order to stabilize it for the time being, before getting it x-rayed later and having a cast put on it.

"A cast?!" I cried, but I can't have that; I've got to go back to school and play goalkeeper for my university soccer team!"

"Not this season you won't!" was his professional reply.

Pain is often an indication of something going on much deeper inside of us. Or pain can be a warning to us that we are pushing our boundaries, whether physical, emotional or even spiritual, beyond where they are meant to be set in order to function properly and in a healthy way. Of course I was completely free to ski the moguls along with everyone else; I was also free to listen to my body, heed the warnings from my lower back and ski alongside the moguls on the smoother part of the slope.

"Everything is permissible—— but not everything is beneficial," wrote Paul to the Corinthians, and in my case, it was completely permissible for me to tackle the moguls, but it certainly wasn't beneficial. (1 Corinthians 10:23 NIV) In addition, pushing the limits, which I often think will bring me more freedom...I want to "break out" of what I perceive as limiting boundaries...ended up costing me dearly. Not only was I limited to skiing the rest of the day with only one ski pole, but also I would be put in a cast for six weeks, completely limiting my life, and radically changing our entire soccer teams' season.

Sometimes we forget that not listening to God's warnings will not only affect us, but many, many others around us. We need to grow in our intimacy with Him to such a point that we hear His warnings, we understand that His warnings are for our good and ultimately, for our freedom, and for the good and freedom of those around us as well, and then we need to heed His warnings. A no-fail path to true freedom in Jesus, especially when His warnings come, is living in an intimate relationship with the Lord, rooted in His Word and in worship; listening to His voice through the Word, teaching and prayer; hearing His Truth through His Holy Spirit; staying in a posture of repentance, forgiveness and blessing; knowing Him and His voice; understanding that He is good all the time, and obeying Him.

That day on the slopes was changed for everyone, not just me. We were not able to stay together as a group and enjoy our final day together. My dad and I had to go to the car and "doctor" my hand. I became the center of attention and concern. My freedom was limited as were some others' all as a result of my bad choices and not listening to God's warnings. The price we pay for not listening can be extremely costly; listening to and obeying Him is always worth it in the end.

Questions to consider:

1. In what areas of your life have you not heeded God's warnings? What has been the result for you and for others?

2. What does 1 John 1:9 teach us about the Lord's heart toward us?

Chapter 12

Pruning and Freedom

My apartment in Szeged, Hungary was located on a very busy downtown street along which grow trees, spaced about 10 feet apart. Two of these trees provide wonderful shade from the blazing afternoon sun which streams in my living room windows and one of the bedroom windows. Szeged is known as the city of sunshine, and so having these trees in front are a wonderful blessing as air-conditioning is quite a luxury and not very common in these old buildings. I live on the first floor, which is actually the second floor by American standards, which lets you know that these trees are rather large and tall, definitely tall enough to provide not only shade but also some privacy and a bit of noise control.

Two years ago, I awakened to the sound of chainsaws. I realized they were not working out back, where there were plenty of trees, but instead, workmen were making their way down the street "trimming" all the trees which lined our street. I had noticed that some of the branches had indeed grown to the point where they were beginning to interfere with the electrical wires that the trolleys run on, so it seemed logical to me that they would be trimming back the branches. However, what I saw defied logic and, for me, the absolute ignoramus when it comes to trees, was absurd and completely destructive.

These tree experts were not simply trimming back longer branches; they were cutting every branch on every tree all the way back to the trunk! They left absolutely nothing...no shoots, no branches, no leaves, nothing. Once they finished with one tree, there stood a tall, bare trunk which looked a bit like a dull pencil tip with a very bad case of acne. As they chain-sawed their way through the two trees directly in front of my flat, the light and heat came pouring through my windows and I felt strangely "exposed" as I looked out on two sickly looking bare trunks standing straight and tall, but appearing very weak and exposed rather than majestic, strong, and full of life.

"You have got to be kidding me!" was all I could muster when I walked outside and saw the extreme pruning continuing on down the street. Full, leafy, strong branches lay helpless at the base of each tree, waiting for the pick-up truck to come and haul them away. I truly thought that maybe some horrible tree disease had hit all the trees on our street and they were taking the first step in tree removal. I fully expected them to return a couple of days later with some huge contraption to uproot all these trees which, to my untrained eye, looked dead. Little did I know, but later I learned, that this is exactly what you do with these particular trees. Every several years, they get completely stripped clean, bare, and branchless, so that they can grow even stronger, healthier, and larger!

In John's gospel, chapter 15, we read about the vine and the branches. Jesus says, "I am the true vine, and my Father is the gardener. He cuts off every branch in me that bears no fruit, while every branch that does bear fruit he prunes so that it will be even more fruitful." (verses 1-2 NIV) The Lord reminded me of this passage as I watched them cut back these trees. However, I usually think of God's pruning as cutting a dead twig off here, a weak branch off there; I never really even considered that God might have to strip absolutely everything, leaving just the "heart" of the individual in order for Him to do what He needs to do to enable her to grow.

Have you experienced a complete and total stripping like these trees or maybe it just "felt" like God had taken the chainsaw and cut away absolutely everything, leaving you exposed and feeling almost naked? I have, and it's not fun.

I later learned that if they did not completely strip these trees like they do, they would not grow properly and would actually become sickly and may die. This physical picture serves as a tremendous object lesson for us who are followers of Jesus. Each of us must be willing to allow God to come and do His stripping, and it could very well mean complete exposure, even though we may not think that is necessary.

God will never over-ride a person's will. As Jesus taught us to pray, "Your will be done on earth as it is in heaven," (Matthew 6:10 NIV) and even in the Garden of Gethsemane, He cried out to His Father in heaven, "Yet not as I will, but as you will." (Matthew 26:39 NIV) God knows best; He knows that if he leaves something untouched, then that thing can cause us not to grow properly in some area of our lives, be it emotionally, physically, or spiritually. In fact, leaving something could actually mean us becoming sick in any of these areas as well. Pruning, the exposure that results and the time that it takes for God to cause new, healthier, stronger growth to emerge, are all crucial elements in walking in freedom.

Along another vein, remember I said that I thought this was the first step in complete tree removal? Well, how many of us, when a brother or sister in Christ is being stripped clean by God Himself jump to the conclusion that there must be something really wrong with that person; he or she must have committed some horrific sin and needs to be removed, or we need to distance ourselves from that person. Sometimes we see part of the picture, or we know one side of the story, and we draw our own conclusions based on that, rather than asking the Lord what is true, as well as hearing the other person's side, and thus seeing the entire picture.

There are always three sides to every story: one person's, the other person's, and the truth, which is God's version. How many of us hear one side, (see only the pruning going on without finding out what the *true Pruner is* actually doing and why) and decide that for whatever reason, that person's side of the story must be correct. Maybe we've known this person longer, or we haven't been in relationship with that person long enough to know if this is really true or not. Or maybe we simply don't want to jeopardize anything, or we're simply too busy to deal with it, and so we don't even bother to find out if what has been said or done is really the truth or really the best way to do things.

Broken relationships within the body of Christ are a sad and, apparently, growing reality. It is often connected to how we are dealing with offense. If we allow offense to enter, anger and resentment follow and can sometimes masquerade as a passion for holiness. Some people wash their hands quickly of association with a fallen individual, trying to clear their name from any connection to them or the situation. Interestingly, Jesus did everything <u>but</u> that.

I saw what the pruners were doing and jumped to a completely wrong conclusion. Oh how often we can do that in our Christian lives as well! This never leads to freedom because the moment we do, we become ensnared by our limited perspective and even more importantly, we run the serious risk of falling into judgment. We must cry out to the One who can give us the truth: God Himself. More importantly, we must realize that but for the grace of God, there go I.

Finally, I said that I too felt rather exposed; and maybe God is doing some pruning of others in your life, sometimes not just pruning them, but completely removing them to expose what is really in both of you! They may have been a source of protection or comfort, but God wants to be your sole source of protection and comfort, and so He allows this to be exposed in you for your own good. Maybe they are removed for a season, but maybe for a lifetime, and it can be painful, like seeing these pitiful looking trunks along my street; and it can appear to be extreme, but His ways are always best and always produce freedom and growth if we will submit to the working of His Holy Spirit within us.

All the trees along my street have grown full, healthy, strong branches and look even better than they did before. I set before us the challenge to let God do His full pruning in our lives, not withholding any branch, but instead, fully submitting to His perfect will, and watching Him set us free to grow stronger than we have ever been in His perfect love, grace and mercy!

"I am the vine; you are the branches. If a person remains in me and I in him, he will bear much fruit; apart from me you can do nothing. This is to my Father's glory, that you bear much fruit..." (John 15: 5, 8 NIV)

I also wish to challenge us to consider when God is busily pruning others that we show love, grace, mercy, acceptance and forgiveness, which sets not only them free, but also us free to continue walking in loving relationship with our Heavenly Father and with each other! Jesus said, "By this all men will know that you are my disciples, if you love one another." (John 13:35 NIV)

Questions to consider:

1. What pruning has the Lord done in your life recently? How have you responded to His "chainsaw"?

2. How have you responded to others whom the Lord is pruning?

Chapter 13

Freedom Through Experiencing Bitterness

"Most assuredly, I say to you, unless a grain of wheat falls into the ground and dies, it remains alone, but if it dies, it produces much grain." (John 12:24 NKJV)

One evening, I swallowed a capsule, but after I swallowed it, I got the distinct feeling that it hadn't gone all the way down. However, I simply ignored it, thinking it would eventually slide down. Then a burp came and up came the now "open" capsules' contents with a burning and bitterness so intense that tears welled up in my eyes. I ran for my water glass and downed it, but the stinging still remained and even intensified as tears rolled down my cheeks. I grabbed something to eat, quickly, and as I swallowed, I could feel the sting, but now a bit less intensively.

So, I continued eating and drinking, trying desperately to get this burning, bitter sensation out of my throat. It lingered for hours, reminding me of what I'd "ignored", and as a result, became a distraction.

God gives us simple warnings all the time. His instructions are perfect, but if we only do something half-way, then the consequences can be intensely uncomfortable. Like the capsule, if I only "partially" or half-heartedly forgive someone rather than forgiving him completely, the bitterness of unforgiveness will come back to sting me somehow. No amount of trying to ease the sting will change the reality that I've not completely forgiven that individual. The clincher in all of this is that I'm the one "burned" and suffering from the "bitter pill"—the other could be miles away, completely unaware and totally unaffected. Unforgiveness *and* forgiveness affect the forgiver—the former keeping one in bitter bondage and the latter setting the forgiver completely free.

When I keep my hands around someone else's throat, which is what unforgiveness is doing, this becomes a distraction for me as well. I'm so focused on the pain, on the unjustness, on what that person or those people have done, that these thoughts consume me and distract me from what God has for me right in front of me, which is first, the truth that He has already forgiven us, and second that we are commanded to forgive others or else our sins will not be forgiven us.

"But if you do not forgive men their trespasses, neither will your Father forgive your trespasses." (Matthew 6:15 NKJV)

We could even conclude that this bitter capsule, called unforgiveness, will remain lodged in our own throat, not just distracting us, but bringing pain and great discomfort.

In the movie *Tuesdays with Morrie*, Morrie says with tremendous conviction: "Forgive everybody everything!" He lived out the end of his days in that film with such freedom and joy, even in the midst of his physical pain, I believe in part because of this biblical truth he lived by: Forgive and you will be forgiven. As he was dying, and as we die to ourselves and live for Jesus alone, he lived more fully than some healthy people; and we too can live and produce much fruit for God's glory!

I've had to swallow some bitter pills in my lifetime, all connected with relationships. Often, there was tremendous misunderstanding which, of course, I always wanted to rectify. Some of these people from one situation came to the forefront of my mind one morning and the bitterness, like that capsule, began to fill my mind and spirit. I began searching for ways to get rid of the pain, the bitterness, and finally cried out to God, "Lord, what should I do? I'm at the end of my rope and I have no clue what I should do! You have to tell me!" I heard the Lord whisper to me in my spirit, "Do nothing!"

When we plant a grain of wheat, it truly "does nothing"; the soil, water and nutrients, as well as the sunshine, act upon that seed, which must "die" in the ground, and only then will it produce much grain. Of course my flesh cried out in rebellion – do nothing—ha! But God's overwhelmingly gracious peace settled deeply in my spirit at that moment as I allowed those two words to sink in: ***Do nothing***. The tears flowed, and the pain and sting remained for a few moments, but God's peace flooded my heart as I released the grip I had on all these peoples' throats and spoke out loud: "I forgive you, I forgive you, I forgive you."

As the water and food coated my capsule burning throat and slowly relieved me of the bitterness of the broken capsule, so speaking forgiveness aloud and releasing these people into the Father's hands permitted God to come in and flood my heart with His forgiveness and peace, removing the bitterness and setting me free. As I continue to die to myself and my flesh, He will bring forth much fruit by His Holy Spirit, for His glory!

Questions to consider:

1. Ask the Father if there is anyone whom you have not forgiven. Can you forgive them now and set *yourself* free?

2. In practical ways, what does it mean to forgive and release those who have hurt us?

Chapter 14

Freedom Emerging Out of the Fiery Furnace

One evening, I had a difficult phone call with a friend. My purely emotional reaction was hurt, betrayal and a profound sense of sadness. I went to bed, hoping a good night's sleep would be restorative. I awakened, wide awake, at 2:30 a.m., heavy-hearted. I wanted to talk to someone, to have someone to pray with and for me, when the Lord gently reminded me: *You can talk to Me!*

As I prayed, I asked God to give me *something* from His Word. He said, "Daniel 3, especially verses 24-25." I turned on the light and opened my Bible, not knowing Daniel 3. I began reading the whole chapter, and when I reached verse 24 where Nebudchadnezzar "leaps up" and sees not *three* men in the fiery furnace but *four*, and the fourth looks like a "son of the gods," tears nearly leapt from my eyes; the Lord gently said, "I am with you in *your* fiery furnace right now." I bawled and bawled, confessing my sin, repenting for not believing that indeed God willingly walks into the fiery furnace He's allowed us to be tossed into, and it's out of the fiery furnace that He is bringing forth His purified gold!

The story in Daniel continues with the King calling Shadrach, Meshach and Abednego to come out of the furnace, and they are completely unharmed, without even a hint of smoke or burn, even on their clothing. However, what the King declares next is simply astounding. In a nation which just a few hours earlier forbade a person from worshipping any other god besides the statue of the King himself, a radical freedom unfolded. "Therefore I decree that the people of any nation or language who say anything against the God of Shadrach, Meshach and Abednego be cut into pieces and their houses be turned into piles of rubble, for no other god can save in this way." (Daniel 3:29 NIV)

When we are seemingly tossed unjustly into whatever fiery furnace that may await us, not only can we know and believe that God is right there with us, as He promises never to leave us or forsake us, but also that a new kind of freedom is going to emerge that could have incredible impact not just on our lives but on those around us and even extending to the nations!

If God's gentle promise to me was not enough, after just four hours of sleep, I walked into school with a supernaturally renewed love and compassion for my students, and teaching was such joy! After school, I took some trousers to the seamstress across the street from my flat and the Lord opened the door for me to tell her about how much Jesus loves her! Her eyes filled with tears, which she held back, but she knew I spoke of a freedom that she desired deep in her heart.

Finally, the next night, I got to hear a fiery furnace story from a dear friend of mine who shared how she was suffering terribly from an inner ear inflammation. When she asked the Lord to show her if there was anything in her life she needed to deal with, and He said, "Yes, you are full of envy!" Immediately, the Lord showed her enviousness and she began confessing and repenting, asking the Lord to forgive her, and at that moment, the horrible pain and inflammation started to subside, very rapidly, along with another seven-month-long excruciatingly painful physical problem. More freedom, Lord!

Out of the fiery furnace, God brings forth His gold, which He is refining for His glory. Are we willing to forsake all, worship Him alone, risk being thrown bound into the fiery furnace? We can be if we see God for who He really is….one who is *in* the fiery furnace with us, bringing us out, and continuing to do His refining work in and through us. His heart's desire is that our hearts would willingly welcome His changing us into healed, healthy living testimonies speaking His freedom and forgiveness into the lives of the ones He loves.

Questions to consider:

1. What fiery furnaces has the Lord allowed you to experience? How have you responded during these tests of your faith?

2. In what ways has your faith been refined like gold?

Part III

Life's Tests of Freedom and Forgiveness

Chapter 15

Freedom and Peace in Brokenness

I sat in my living room quietly checking my emails when I heard a loud crash come from the kitchen. My younger brother and his family were visiting me and they were eating breakfast in my kitchen which only holds about three people comfortably, four if you don't mind having no elbow room. Obviously, the elbow room had run out, and some minor disaster had taken place. I stopped typing long enough to ask, from a distance, "What happened?"

"An entire glass of fruit smoothie fell on the floor and shattered! We're so sorry!" I didn't move, and continued reading emails, responding with, "That's ok. Don't worry about it."

"Do you have a mop we can clean this up with and a broom and dustpan?"

"Sure," I responded, amazingly nonchalantly. I surprised myself with my casual response to the situation. I got up and gave them the clean-up items, and then returned to my computer.

"We'll buy you a new glass...we're so sorry!"

"There is no need for that," I answered. "I have more than enough glasses as you can see! Really, it's no big deal! Let it go!"

Let it go. Let it go. Let it go.

Ok, for any of you who know me, this was not like me. I guess I should say, this is not like the Arden that used to be. I can honestly say that I was not ruffled one bit by this incident. For me not to jump up and help, or insist that I clean it up, or be concerned is an Arden that is now even foreign to me. I don't quite "get it", but finally, about a month after this incident, the Lord graciously showed me His perspective. It came during a time of reading God's Word and prayer, when I sensed in my spirit the Lord speaking these words to me:

"You, Arden, have experienced such brokenness in the past years and especially the past year, and in this tangible way, you are that broken, shattered glass, and everything in you has been poured out. However, instead of you trying to rush in and clean yourself up and stress out about what's happened, you have allowed ME to come in and begin cleaning up the mess."

Wow! That's the only response I could muster when this revelation came pouring in. Why? Because like a lot of people I know, I knew that I had tried to fix things and had tried to change myself; yet having gotten no where, I finally gave up and let God be

Walking Forward

God. When I did that, the cleaning up and healing began.

I asked a friend for her perspective on all of this as well because of this sort of "numbness" I've been experiencing emotionally; her response was the biggest revelation quite possibly of my life. "Oh yea, I know that sort of numb feeling and I asked God about it and He told me, 'That's peace.'"

Another jolt. Peace?

Simple as that? This calm, non-stressed, non-reactive, seemingly uncaring, feeling sort of numb state of being is God's peace? My friend's statement resonated deeply within me, and the most amazing part was realizing that quite possibly, I'd never really known God's peace, even though I'd walked with God for more than 25 years? Maybe I'd had snippets of peace, but this deep, abiding, residing, calm that has settled in…this is the peace that passes all understanding because surely, I don't understand it.

However, it has come at a tremendous cost: being broken and shattered and everything within being poured out. It has cost becoming a mess, or rather recognizing that I am a mess, and allowing God to enter in and make all things new, in His way, in His time and pour in His peace. Broken, shattered, weak and needy, I am free to be healed, restored and empowered by the only one able to do it thoroughly, completely and perfectly—God Himself! "Therefore, if anyone is in Christ, he is a new creation; the old has gone, the new has come! All this is from God, who reconciled us to himself through Christ…" (2 Corinthians 5:17 NIV)

Questions to consider:

1. How do you often respond when something goes wrong or "gets broken"?

2. How does brokenness lead to peace?

3. Find as many verses as you can which speak about God's peace and write them out below.

Chapter 16

Freedom – Knowing the Whole Story

I received a notice in my post-box in Hungary stating that I needed to go to the post office to pick up a registered letter from the police. I immediately thought, "Oh wow, I know exactly what this is!" A few nights earlier, I had pulled onto my street right behind a police car, and the policeman inside immediately turned on his flashing lights for me to pull over. I pulled into the driveway leading into the courtyard of the building where I lived and rolled down my window. He asked for my license, my residency permit, my address card, my car papers and my permission to park in my enclosed courtyard area, off the street. I lived on a restricted street where only buses, trolleys and taxis may go, unless one lived on this street and, as I learned that night, had special permission to drive there and park there.

Since I didn't know I had to have permission, I jumped to the conclusion that *this* is what the letter must be about. I was being fined for coming down this street!

When I opened the letter, I saw the "check" attached to it that I must pay and the fine was $160! I tried to read the letter, which was in Hungarian, saw the word "permission" and concluded that my run-in with the police a few nights earlier had earned me this fine. I even took the letter to two other people, Hungarians, who, having briefly glanced at it, said they too had gotten such a punishment and fine. We discussed things and 'concluded' that this seemed like a very steep fine, etc.

Finally, I faxed the letter to another friend, requesting his help in dealing with this situation, due to the fact that I'd not known I ***needed*** permission to park inside the yard! I wanted to try to get the fine reduced or dismissed altogether due to lack of information given to me.

My friend called me after having received my fax and said, "Arden, I'm afraid to tell you this, but this is a speeding ticket!"

"What?" I asked.

"It looks like you were speeding on the new bridge," my friend explained.

I picked up the letter that was sitting on the desk next to me and I TURNED IT OVER—

AHA! THERE'S A PAGE TWO!

AHA! THERE'S ANOTHER SIDE!

Clearly written on the other side was that a speed gun and camera had caught me going 72 kilometers/

hour in a 50 kilometers/hour zone nearly a month earlier! Oops, guilty as charged!

Now everything was clear! *Now* I had the whole picture! *Now* I knew the whole story! *Now* the clarity of the situation and my guilt was established.

The Lord opened my eyes through this situation to a lesson, I believe, from which everyone can benefit. I know a group of people, and maybe you do too, who have received a kind of 'letter'. They have half the information. With half the information, they, like I did, have drawn their own conclusions based on page-one information. The problem is that there is a page two. None of them has turned the 'letter' over to read page two. The result has been wrong conclusions, which have led to sad and disastrous results, broken relationships and much hurt, more far-reaching than the immediate situation.

What these people need to do is turn the 'letter' over and read the other side. With **all** the information, they can then draw true and accurate conclusions. Their ultimate choices may not change, but at least there would be full disclosure. As it stands now, they are in a kind of bondage, so to say, imprisoned by the limited information they have. Their imprisonment has kept them and others from experiencing both the forgiveness and the freedom that can emerge through reconciliation and restoration.

How often do we in the body of Christ 'read only one side of the letter', bring our preconceived notions into a situation and draw inaccurate conclusions based on half the story? How many people have we hurt in the process? How much unity in the

Kingdom of God has been severed as a result? How much 'work' for the Kingdom has not gone forward as a result of such situations? How many people are the victims of us imprisoning them by only knowing and/or seeking out part of the story? How many of us are victims of such imprisonment?

I have no excuse for not having turned over the letter from the police to read all the information. Truly, it was silly of me to be so careless not to notice there was another side to the letter. Likewise, I have no excuse when I listen to only one side of a story and draw conclusions based on half the information. I am guilty of having done this before, and I have had to repent in tears for the hurt, disappointment and brokenness I've caused other people.

So too I've found myself on the receiving end of such actions, when others have read one side of the 'letter' and not turned it over to read the other. Sadly, this has happened with fellow Christian believers. For me, that has been the more challenging scenario because in some situations, all communication was broken between me and them with no door left open for any chance at biblical reconciliation. However, God, in His loving mercy, made it clear that I am to forgive, and cry out just as Jesus did from the cross, "Father, forgive them for they do not know what they are doing." (Luke 23:34 NIV)

I am commanded to forgive. As I have forgiven and blessed those who are one-side-of-the-letter-readers, a wonderful thing has happened: I've been set free! Yes, some sadness and disappointment remains because of broken relationships, but mostly because they don't know what they are doing. As it was with those who misinterpreted Jesus, some people only read what they choose to read, and they only listen to what they choose to listen to, instead of turning the page to read the whole story.

Jesus faced these kinds of people when He was here on earth. "You diligently study the Scriptures because you think that by them you possess eternal life. These are the Scriptures that testify about Me, yet you refuse to come to Me to have life." (John 5:38-40 NIV) These people had God's law and the prophets and studied them diligently. They knew this part of God's Word; but they refused to turn the page and recognize the Word of Life, about whom and to whom all the Law and the Prophets testified and pointed. Had they read page two, they would know the One who could bring full understanding and set them free to be in living, loving relationship with their heavenly Father.

What hindered them? Pride? Desire for control? Lies whispered to them from the enemy? Their own flesh? Fear? Ignorance? More importantly, what keeps us from reading page two?

Just as the Pharisees and Sadducees tried to defend themselves, only reading the first page and drawing their own conclusions about Jesus, I wanted to defend myself regarding this letter from the police. However, it turns out the Pharisees and Sadducees and I were all guilty. And maybe in the body of Christ, this conclusion is reached in many situations once the whole 'letter' is read. But maybe the opposite could be true in any given situation. We assume somebody is 'guilty' but then turn the page to see that he or she is not, or that, at the very least, there is another perspective. Regardless of the situation, a vital key is to let God be God and deal with each individual heart as only He is able, which is always perfectly. I have forgiven in situations where half-truths and one side of the story have been told. I have also had to ask for forgiveness. In most cases, people have read the other side of the letter, responded with God's grace and have forgiven me. Beautiful supernatural healing and restoration has occurred in each of those situations as forgiveness and the love of God has prevailed and even healthier relationships have emerged! In other situations, people have chosen not to respond or to forgive. In the latter cases, I have done what I can do, and they must make the choice to turn the 'letter' over, read the whole story, and decide for themselves what God's truth is.

As painful as such realities may be for everyone who has endured such situations, even greater degrees of misguided misunderstandings were faced by our Lord Jesus. He is able, if we will draw close to Him, to guide us into the freedom He experienced in the very midst of people's page-one readings about who He was and even today, who He is. "You don't know me or my Father…if you knew me, you would know my Father also…I am not alone, for my Father is with me." (John 8:19; 16:32 NIV) Jesus knew who He was and whose He was, and He never allowed the one-side-of-the-page readers to ruffle His feathers. When we are faced with these situations, we should keep our eyes fixed on Jesus, lean hard into His love and grace, because he promises, "My grace is sufficient for you, for My power is made perfect in weakness." (2 Corinthians 12:9 NIV)

We may feel weak in the face of page-one readers, but the grace of God is sufficient! Only in that amazing grace through the power and ministry of the Holy Spirit within us are we set free to forgive them, love them and bless them, in Jesus' name!

Questions to consider:

1. Have you ever been a "page-one" reader? How has that affected you?

2. Have you been the victim of "page-one" readers? Have you forgiven those involved and allowed the Lord to set you free? If not, would be willing to do so now?

3. Are there any situations where you need to "let God be God"? Bring those situations to the Lord and release them to Him.

Chapter 17

Freedom to the End!

I recently watched the movie *Brave Heart*, thinking that of course I'd seen it before. However, as the film progressed, I realized I'd probably only seen parts, and I was completely intrigued by the message of freedom which resonates throughout the story, even to the very closing scenes!

For those who may not have seen the film, its main character, William Wallace is a boy born with a passionate heart, who grows into a man of passion and purpose. While still a young boy, William lost his father, who was killed by the English troops invading Scotland at the time. Of course William didn't want to leave his home, and everything that was familiar, but he had to leave and go live with his uncle. Little William grew in every way in the process, and by letting go of the old, all things were made new.

However, William held fast to one "old" thing: his true love for a young girl who selflessly loved him by giving him a flower at his father's funeral.

Deep down, he seemed to know even then that she was the one for him. The boy William rode away with his uncle where he learned different languages and most importantly, according to his uncle, learned to use his head because in doing that, it would direct his heart. Like William's uncle admonished him to use his head, we followers of Jesus "have the mind of Christ" and the Apostle Paul clearly instructs us to "be transformed by the renewing of (our) mind." (Romans 12:2 NIV) It's with the mind of Christ that our hearts follow hard after Him and His purposes in our lives and in this world.

After years of being away, William returns home with the sole desire of settling down, farming, marrying and having a family. He and the love of his youth marry secretly, and they enjoy a short, idyllic time together. Everything lies before them: excitement, joy, love, passion, hopes and dreams. However, in a moment, all of these are smashed as both the flesh and the enemy "team up" to steal, kill and destroy. His young love's throat is ruthlessly slit by the invading English occupiers.

Shortly thereafter, William returns to the village, riding his horse, seemingly unarmed, boasting a position of surrender, arms outstretched; however, in reality, the passion of his heart for ONE THING has been ignited by the senseless murder of his bride: FREEDOM. He pulls from out of the back of his shirt, a long, deadly sword, and kills the English soldier who approaches him on his horse. His boldness in that moment inspires the Scots in that village to stand up against their enemy and defeat them. His sole passion, born out of a wounded heart, is freedom; he has no fear because he knows what is true and what is right.

Sometimes we have to lose that which is most precious to us in this world to be able to see, understand and live for that which, eternally, is even more precious.

William does not simply defend his own territory, but fights to take back what the enemy has stolen. He never compromises and he garners the support he needs, continually reiterating and declaring that unity is the only way to succeed. How very true this is in the Body of Christ as well as we are called to be One Body: "I in them and You in me that the world may believe that You have sent me" (John 17:21 NIV)

On the enemy's side were greed, oppression, sexual immorality, deception and pride. Both kings depicted in the film, the King of England and the King of Scotland, are driven by the flesh and become pawns in the enemy's hands. It is fascinating to watch them both deteriorate physically as the film progresses. Meanwhile, the forces standing for truth grow increasingly stronger.

Just when it seems that those standing with William are a definite force to be reckoned with against the invading English, and the plan is laid for a sure victory, William is abandoned by his own countrymen. They, in the thick of battle, even after promising to stand with him to the end, look him in the eye and turn and ride away. "But it is you, my companion, my close friend, with whom I once enjoyed sweet fellowship..." (Psalm 55:13-14 NIV)

I'm sure there are many of us who have experienced a similar situation, someone stating, like Peter did, "I'll be there for you through thick and thin; I'll be a friend for life; I'll be loyal to you!" Yet in the thick of battle, for whatever reasons, those people turn and walk away, leaving you sickeningly abandoned on the battlefield of life.

William could have easily lost heart, but instead, he turns again with a renewed fire in his eyes to attack the enemy. In our situations, we too can continue on, and must move forward, knowing that He who died for us "will never leave us nor forsake us." (Hebrews 13:5 NIV) We cannot give up simply because friends, family, acquaintances, co-workers, or even brothers and sisters in the church choose to turn their backs. We are called to "fix our eyes on Jesus, the author and perfecter of our faith, who, for the joy set before him endured the cross, scorning its shame and sat down at the right hand of the throne of God." (Hebrews 12:2 NIV) Your cross is different from everyone else's, but take heart because Jesus has borne the heaviest cross of all—every one of our sins!

William does not do what Christ has commanded us to do—he does not forgive those who have wronged him, nor does he bless them. We, however, are commanded by Jesus to do just this: forgive and bless, and I would "add", verbally speak words of blessing over those people in prayer. Of course our flesh wants to do what he did: get revenge. "'It is mine to avenge, I will repay,' says the Lord. On the contrary: 'If your enemy is hungry, feed him; if he is thirsty, give him something to eat.'" (Romans 12:19-20 NIV)

Vengeance, even if it is simply in the form of non-forgiveness, can be deadly and detrimental. God's Word says that if we don't forgive those who have sinned against us, then our Heavenly Father will not forgive us our sins.

I was riding the train with a couple of friends, having a great conversation about various topics when the subject of forgiveness came up. "I will never, ever, ever forgive my father, and you cannot ever convince me to forgive him!" said one of my traveling companions. I sat quietly asking the Lord for His wisdom when He dropped two situations from my own life into my heart to share with her. The first had to do with a friend, whose biological father left the family high and dry when she was only four years old. About two years ago, I broached the subject with this friend, asking if she had ever forgiven her father. "I just try not to think about it." I gently shared with her the truth that forgiveness sets the forgiver free, releasing the forgiver from any "power" that unforgiveness has over them, which can take many forms, such as bitterness, anger, a hard heart, and even physical ailments. There is evidence in Scripture and in the daily lives of people that not forgiving affects us physically.

I then shared an incident that happened to me when I was just an adolescent. Even though I had been very traumatized by it, God had given me the grace in later years, to forgive, and such love and compassion wells up in me when I pray for these people that tears form in my eyes. Both of my friends on the train looked at me incredulously as tears flowed, and the grace of the moment could be tangibly felt. Forgiving those who have betrayed us or hurt us in some way, as this young lady's dad did, is only possible through the blood and grace of Jesus Christ. We are offered the chance to make that choice and choose, by an act of our wills, to forgive. When we do, freedom begins to enter in like never before.

William Wallace encountered extreme betrayal as well when the soon-to-be King of Scotland, who pledged his loyalty to William "to the end", becomes a complete turn-coat. He hides behind a helmet that disguises him, but when the steel helmet is ripped off, by William himself, and he is exposed, William cannot kill him. The betrayal is too unbelievable. Instead, William totally loses spirit, and for the first time, he does not rise and fight, but lays back in disbelief.

Very probably you've had someone who pledged loyalty to you but then, influenced by whatever has "entered in"—the flesh, sin, the enemy or a combination—that person completely turned on you. The very life was sapped out of you; you cannot believe that THIS person, out of everyone, would do such a thing. Or maybe YOU have been the one behind the steel helmet. Either way there is excruciating pain which you have endured or which you have caused. The pain, as seen on William's face, seems unbearable, but we as followers of Jesus have to cling to the cross and bring all of that pain to Him because He truly does care for us! (1 Peter 5:7 NIV).

We as believers can only hope in the God of hope and pray that the conviction which we see hit Robert's heart of how he has sinned and hurt someone so deeply will also hit the hearts of those who have hurt us, or our hearts if we have hurt others. When godly conviction comes, then repentance, forgiveness and healing will begin. This is where we must let God be God and He will do His work in them, and in us.

Robert confronts his earthly father who had, earlier, subtly convinced him to walk down this path of betrayal, and in this scene, we see his father's face completely eaten away with leprosy. Once Robert sees who the REAL enemy is and what the TRUTH really is, he rejects the evil lies and embraces truth. Yet, there are deadly consequences.

William is captured and faces torture. He is given the opportunity to bow his knee to the "enemy", the invading King of England, but refuses to do so, and therefore faces brutal public humiliation, torture and finally, death. In his prison cell, William is clearly a Christ-figure as he is seen praying, saying, "I'm so afraid! Give me Your strength!" He refuses the sedative to numb the pain he will endure because he will experience the full force of the torture inflicted, just as Jesus experienced the full weight of our sin. Instead of crying out "Mercy", thus pledging allegiance to the enemy, he cries out, with everything within him, "FREEDOM!"

Our Lord cried out from the cross, "Father, forgive them for they do not know what they are doing." (Luke 23:34 NIV) Thus, He ushered in, through the cross and resurrection on the third day, the greatest freedom the human race has ever known since the fall of man in the garden.

Forgiveness sets the forgiver free, and it's only when we forgive those who have hurt us deeply that we will be able to shout, even in the midst of extreme pain, "FREEDOM!" We can cry out like the Psalmist: "Teach me your way, O Lord; lead me in a straight path because of my oppressors. Do not turn me over to the desire of my foes, for false witnesses rise up against me, breathing out violence. I am still confident of this: I will see the goodness of the Lord in the land of the living. Wait for the Lord; be strong and take heart and wait for the Lord." (Psalm 27:12-14 NIV)

When friends become like enemies for whatever reason, we are called to do four specific things:

"Love your enemies";
"Do good to those who hate you";
"Bless those who curse you";
"Pray for those who mistreat you". (Luke 6:27-28)

How do we love our enemies? First, we must know that we are utterly and totally loved by our Heavenly Father. Then, we must receive His love into our hearts for ourselves and then too for those who are our "enemies", those who have hurt us. Finally, we must ask the Father to give us His wisdom to know how to love them practically. Let the Holy Spirit be your guide in showing you how to love them. He loves to do this. "I will guide you with my eye." (Psalm 32:8 NKJV)

How do we do good to those who hate us? Once again, this takes wisdom flowing from above. Nurturing a deep intimacy with Jesus is of foremost importance. Learning to hear His voice when praying about and for your enemies and how you are to do good to them will then flow out of your intimate relationship with Him.

Bless those who curse you? This is completely counter-cultural behavior. Only when the Spirit of God flows in and through us will we be able, when cursed or when spoken evil of, to bless those people. Why does God call us to do this? We will reap what we sow. In addition, our perfect example is Jesus hanging on the cross and crying out for forgiveness, as noted above.

Finally, how do we pray for those who mistreat us? I've found the easiest way to do this practically is to pray Scripture verses over those people, especially verses which contain blessings and God's promises. As I do this, God changes my heart, and I find that His love truly is overflowing in me toward them, even if I never get to see them or speak to them again. The day may come when I will stand face to face with those "enemies" or those who have mistreated me, and I pray that God will have so changed me and my heart that nothing but His love, grace and mercy flows out from me to them as a result of dwelling in His presence, in His Word, and in worship! I pray that same mercy will flow toward me from those whom I have mistreated! Grace truly is a two-way street.

Looking at the film *Brave Heart* utterly symbolically, we are indeed to stand firm against the true enemy: Satan, whose invading armies bring lies, deception, destruction, and despair. We are to stand FOR the Truth, which is Jesus, who came to set us free! "It is for freedom that Christ has set us free!" (Galatians 5:1 NIV) We are to forgive and bless those who have hurt us, because only then, do we know true freedom in Christ. "And the peace of God which transcends all understanding will guard our hearts and minds in Christ Jesus! (Philippians 4:7 NIV) If we are the ones who have caused the hurt, we must first ask for forgiveness from the ones we have wronged, and then forgive ourselves, because God has already forgiven us through Jesus! We are called to do all that which is within our power to make things right and be vessels of life-giving, healing forgiveness which sets people free!

Questions to consider:

1. What challenging situations have you faced where you have had to, by an act of your will, chosen to walk in freedom and forgiveness?

2. What is worth living for? Dying for?

Chapter 18

Freedom on the Other Side....

Daily challenges face each of us; so too do opportunities to see the hand of God, hear His voice and obey in the midst of those challenges. Whether you were raised in an excellent family or one where abuse and neglect was the norm, the reality is everyone on the planet is a wounded relative of our first father and mother, Adam and Eve. They were the first to believe lies and act upon them, reaping the consequences. Only through the last Adam, Jesus Christ and his death on the cross and resurrection, do we have the pre-paid ticket to both freedom and forgiveness.

So it's only on the other side of the cross, after we take all of our sin, our judgments, the lies we've believed, the unforgiveness we've harbored and push it into Jesus' nail-pierced hands that we can begin the journey of walking forward into the freedom and

Walking Forward

forgiveness that gives life to us and to those around us. I pray all of us stop drinking poison, waiting for someone else to die, and instead forgive and set ourselves free!

As you remain in close intimate relationship with the Holy Spirit, "Whether you turn to the right or to the left, your ears will hear a voice behind you, saying, 'This is the way; walk in it.'" (Isaiah 31:21 NIV) May the freedom for which Christ set us free be a reality as we walk forward every day, forgive and know the reality of that grace-filled freedom!

LaVergne, TN USA
27 August 2010
194993LV00002B/2/P